A HISTORY OF ANKOLE

A HISTORY OF ANKOLE

H. F. MORRIS

with a Foreword by

Z. C. K. MUNGONYA

FOUNTAIN PUBLISHERS
Kampala

Fountain Publishers Ltd
P. O. Box 488 Kampala
E-mail:sales@fountainpublishers.co.ug
Website:www.fountainpublishers.co.ug

Distributed in Europe, North America and Australia by African Books
Collective Ltd. (ABC), Unit 13, Kings Meadow Oxford OX2 0DP,
United Kingdom. Tel: 44-(0) 1865-726686, Fax:44-(0)1865-793298

© H.F. Morris 1962, 2007
First published 1962
Reprinted 2007

ISBN 978-9970-02-689-0

CONTENTS

FOREWORD

IT GIVES me great pleasure to write the Foreword to this book which takes the history of the Banyankore from earliest legendary times to the year 1914. The material, much of which was originally written by Dr. Morris in former articles for the *Uganda Journal*, provides the first history of the Ankole people to be published in English. Dr. Morris served for three years as a District Officer in Ankole, and then and since made a study of the history and the language of the Banyankore. In fact Dr. Morris is one of very few British officers who have ever become thoroughly fluent in the language of the Banyankore. His profound knowledge of the language made his work in this field easier and enabled him to speak freely and to understand all verbal accounts of past events and history of the period up to 1890, which were given to him by elderly Banyankore who were proud to remember them and to pass them on; many of whom have since died. It is possible that some Banyankore may disagree with some of the old legends or myths in this work, particularly those concerning the Bacwezi, but the Banyankore have an unfailing interest in the old history of their country and the legends and myths which have been written in this work are those generally accepted by the people of Ankole. For this period up to 1890, Dr. Morris has also relied upon oral tradition drawn from published sources such as Messrs. Katate and Kamugungunu's *Abagabe b'Ankole*. To many Banyankore, too little is known about the Abakama of Mpororo, Buhweju, Bunyaruguru, Buzimba and Igara, and this work gives legends concerning them and a very interesting history of these counties as far as is known. It explains how they eventually became incorporated into the Kingdom of Ankole.

For the last twenty years or so of the period covered the main source of material has been the Archives in the Entebbe Secretariat. This work will be of considerable value to all officers working in Ankole and to the Banyankore themselves, and it is to be hoped that it will be widely read. I warmly commend it.

Z. C. K. MUNGONYA
Minister of Lands and Mineral Development

Entebbe,
    12*th April*, 1961.

THE BAHINDA DYNASTY

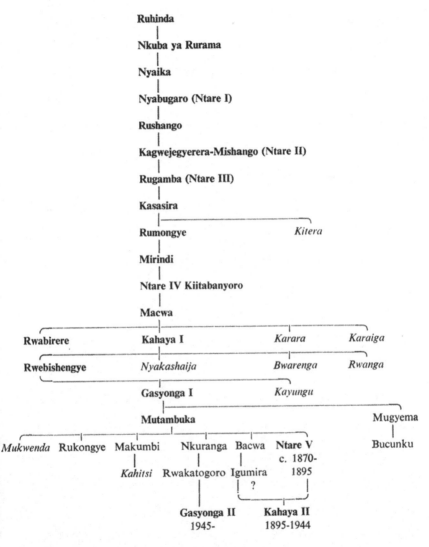

Ruhinda
|
Nkuba ya Rurama
|
Nyaika
|
Nyabugaro (Ntare I)
|
Rushango
|
Kagwejegyerera-Mishango (Ntare II)
|
Rugamba (Ntare III)
|
Kasasira
|
Rumongye   *Kitera*
|
Mirindi
|
Ntare IV Kiitabanyoro
|
Macwa

Rwabirere   **Kahaya I**   *Karara*   *Karaiga*

Rwebishengye   *Nyakashaija*   *Bwarenga*   *Rwanga*

Gasyonga I   *Kayungu*

Mutambuka   Mugyema

Mukwenda   Rukongye   Makumbi   Nkuranga   Bacwa   **Ntare V**   Bucunku
c. 1870-
              Kahitsi   Rwakatogoro   Igumira   1895
                              ?

Gasyonga II   **Kahaya II**
1945-   1895-1944

Note: True Abagabe are in bold type and usurpers (*ebyebumbe*) in italics. In deciding who should rank as real Abagabe I have followed Messrs. Katate and Kamugungunu.[*]

Opinion differs whether Kahaya II was the son of Ntare or Igumira, see page 33.

---

[*] A. G. Katate and L. Kamugungunu, M.B.E. *Abagabe b'Ankole, Ekitabo I & II*, Eagle Press, Kampala, 1955.

Chapter I

INTRODUCTION

THE kingdom of Ankole with its half a million inhabitants has, like the other kingdoms of this part of East Africa, a traditional history handed down orally from generation to generation which extends over many centuries. Of written records, on the other hand, we have nothing until the accounts of the journeys of H. M. Stanley, the first European to set foot in Ankole, in the year 1876. Were it not for the oral traditions which have been preserved, all we could say with any certainty is that at some stage, probably well before the fourteenth century, an Hamitic people, or a series of waves of these people, entered Uganda, coming originally, if not directly, from the north or north-east with their long horned cattle and established their rule upon the existing Bantu cultivators whose language they adopted. On this foundation arose kingdoms with a comparatively well-developed degree of organisation whose rulers were devoted to the possession of cattle.

In the absence of written records, it is to oral tradition that we have to turn in order to discover the story of the development of these kingdoms through the centuries. Many of the traditions of the Banyankore's history have during this century been written down and preserved though so much has, with the passing away of the last generation to remember pre-British times, been lost for ever, and it is upon these accounts of the traditional stories and upon information given to me direct by Banyankore who had been young men when the British Administration was established, that I have relied in piecing together an account of the history of Ankole down to the second half of the nineteenth century.

Since the historian of a people such as the Banyankore is dependent upon oral traditions, it is necessary for him to examine such traditions very closely. He must carefully assess both their value and their limitations and then decide how much reliance he should place upon them. It would be as foolish blindly to accept them in all their details as true historical accounts as it would be to dismiss them as fairy tales unworthy of any belief. The Ankole traditions deal with three stages in the people's development. First, there are the stories of the dynasty of pre-Bacwezi kings. Here we are dealing completely with myths and not with facts, with stories which account for the origin of the people and tell of their supernatural rulers and which bear many similarities to those which other races throughout

1

the world have preserved of their creation. Here we are told of the first king, Ruhanga (the Creator), who came down from heaven whither he later returned, and of his three sons Kakama, Kahima and Kairu who represent the three divisions of the Banyankore people, the ruling clan, the pastoral Bahima and the agriculturist Bairu, each with its own part to play in society.

There follow the accounts of the second dynasty, the Bacwezi. Here opinion is divided as to whether these tales of the members of a wondrous clan who established a vast kingdom, which they ruled for a couple of generations, and then mysteriously departed, are or are not founded on historical fact. C. C. Wrigley maintains that here too we are dealing entirely with myths; that these tales give gods human forms and tell of their story in human terms; that, for example, the Bunyoro legend of Isaza who descended into the underworld is "a splendid piece of fantasy woven round the setting of the sun".[1] Most writers, however, support the view—in my opinion the more likely—that the Bacwezi were an historical dynasty, a superior race of immigrants who imposed their will over a very wide area and whose rule, for reasons at which we can only guess, later came abruptly to an end. On account, however, of the might and superior culture of these Bacwezi rulers, their memory was, according to this theory, preserved and later generations of their former subjects worshipped them, thereafter, as their gods. The stories of these mysterious people and the cult of their worship are known not only throughout almost all western Uganda but also in the Lake Province of Tanganyika as far south as Tabora. Various theories have been suggested as to who these Bacwezi were; it has been put forward that they were partly of Portuguese origin, emigrants from Abyssinia where the Portuguese had established themselves in the sixteenth century[2] and it has even been suggested that they may have been the descendants of a lost Roman army. Father Crazzolara, on the other hand, has argued that they were Nilotes.[3] The most plausible explanation, however, is that they and their followers formed one of the Hamitic influxes into Uganda and Tanganyika and that they did not differ essentially in race from the Hamitic Bahima who, according to traditional accounts, were already in the country. Further archaeological research at places such as Bigo bya Mugenyi which are traditionally associated with the Bacwezi may confirm or contradict this supposition, but preliminary investigations carried out at Bigo so far suggest its occupation by a people with a culture not materially different from that of the Bahima.[4]

---

1 C. C. Wrigley "Some Thoughts on the Bacwezi", *Uganda Journal*, Vol. 22, 1958.
2 Father J. Nicolet, *Mucondozi*, Mbarara, 1953.
3 Father J. P. Crazzolara, *The Lwoo, Part I*, Verona, 1950.
4 P. L. Shinnie "Excavations at Bigo", *Uganda Journal*, Vol. 24, 1960.

Then we have the accounts of the Bahinda dynasty. Here we are on much surer ground and we can assume that we are dealing with a record which is basically an authentic factual account of the fortunes of the Omugabe's kingdom and its development from small beginnings until, some three centuries later, it became the dominant power in what is now Ankole district. These traditional accounts can, to a certain extent, be checked with the accounts of neighbouring tribes and references will be found to the same events in the oral traditions of different kingdoms. There will, for example, be found references both in Ankole and in Bunyoro traditions to invasions of Ankole by the Abakama Olimi I and Cwamali of Bunyoro and comparisons of the genealogies of the two ruling houses show that both people place these invasions at about the same date. There is, however, a danger here which must not be overlooked. It may be that one tribe has borrowed the traditions of another or adapted their own traditions in the light of those of a neighbouring people.

Another more certain, but as yet less profitable, means whereby tradition can be checked is archaeological research. Comparatively little of this research has, as yet, been done in Uganda but I should like to refer to one interesting discovery made by Dr. Posnansky during the excavation of a traditional site of an Omugabe's palace at Bweyorore which illustrates my point very well. Traditional accounts vary regarding the Omugabe connected with the site. According to one source Macwa, who reigned in the middle of the eighteenth century, had his palace there, but according to another the site was connected with Kasasira, who reigned about a century earlier.[5] Here was apparent conflict which suggested that oral tradition was an unreliable source. When Bweyorore[6] was excavated, however, evidence was found of two periods of occupation on the same site which could well have been separated by one hundred years. Thus were the two conflicting traditional accounts confirmed and reconciled.

To attempt to determine dates from oral tradition is a risky undertaking, but, provided the margin of error to which any such calculations are liable is allowed for, a rough guide is provided for us by the traditional genealogies which have been preserved. A comparison between the genealogies of the ruling families of Ankole, Buganda and Bunyoro shows roughly the same number of generations covering the same period of time, that is to say, from the break-up of the Bacwezi kingdom till the end of the nineteenth century, Ankole allowing for seventeen generations, Buganda for eighteen and Bunyoro for seventeen. It is, of course, possible that, for

---

5 R. Oliver "Ancient Capital Sites of Ankole", *Uganda Journal*, Vol. 23, 1959.
6 Bweyorore lies about one mile east of the Mbarara-Kikagati road, seventeen miles from Mbarara. Excavations were carried out in 1959 by Dr. Posnansky, Curator of the Uganda Museum.

reasons of tribal pride, each kingdom has tried to make its pedigree as long as it can and has added to it so that it should not appear shorter than those of its neighbours. Provided, however, that this has not happened, then the similarity between these figures suggests that the pedigrees are fairly accurate. It is also reasonable to presume that, on an average, there will be four generations to a century, that is to say that each Omugabe through the centuries was on an average born when his father was about twenty-five years old. This means to say that the eighteen generations which separate the present Omugabe from his ancestor Ruhinda cover a period of about four and a half centuries and that the latter was probably reigning at some time during the fifteenth century. Since, however, the possibility of error becomes greater the longer the period in respect of which such a calculation is made, any date fixed by these means as far back as the fifteenth century cannot be accepted as being likely to be at all accurate.[7] Occasionally we are fortunate enough to have some external evidence by which these calculations can be checked. The obvious example is the traditional Buganda story that, during the reign of the Kabaka Juko, an eclipse of the sun took place. Now, according to a reckoning by generations, Juko would have been living towards the end of the seventeenth century, whilst it is known scientifically that an eclipse of the sun which would have been visible in Buganda took place in the year 1680.[8] Using this firm date of 1680 as a base, we can then fix reasonably accurately the dates of the rulers of neighbouring kingdoms who were Juko's near contemporaries. According to both Ankole and Bunyoro traditions, Ntare Kiitabanyoro was a contemporary of Cwamali against whom he fought. Cwamali's grandfather, Winyi II, is said to have been a contemporary of the Buganda Kabaka Katarega, Juko's father, whilst Cwamali's son, Kyebambe I, was a contemporary of the Kabaka Kagulu, Juko's grandson. This strongly suggests that Cwamali and Ntare were one generation after Juko and implies that Ntare's accession would have taken place about the year 1700, which agrees with the date that a calculation by generations from the Ankole pedigree would fix.

It is important to bear in mind that the kingdom which the Bahinda Abagabe established on the break-up of the Bacwezi's rule, which was known first as Kaaro-Karungi and later as Nkore, was originally very

---

7 R. Oliver in "Ancient Capital Sites", *op. cit.*, has devised a formula for assessing the dates of the Abagabe based on the assumption that, since the heir of a deceased Omugabe would be chosen from the sons who were born after his succession to the throne, the generations would be rather longer than normal, and that a generation should be reckoned on an average of twenty-seven years. He further makes an allowance for a margin of error of two years plus or minus for each generation, a margin of error which would amount to over half a century in the case of Ruhinda's dates.

8 J. M. Gray "Early History of Buganda", *Uganda Journal*, Vol. 2, 1935.

small in area, and even at the beginning of the eighteenth century comprised little more than the present saza of Isingiro. It was not until the eighteenth and nineteenth centuries that the Abagabe, benefiting from the decline of Bunyoro and the break-up of Mpororo, extended their rule north and west. Even by the time of Ntare V's death, the Abagabe, although they had established their control over many other petty states, exercised direct rule only over the eastern part of the present district of Ankole. It was only after the first government station had been opened at Mbarara in 1898 that the outlying kingdoms such as Buhweju and Igara were incorporated in that of the Omugabe and included in the administrative district of Ankole, the name of which is a European corruption of Nkore.[9] A history of Ankole must therefore record not only the development of the Omugabe's kingdom of Nkore but also of the other component parts of the present district. I have accordingly, in the following chapters, begun with a summary of the early legends which are common to most of the Western Province people, though the version I have given is the Ankole one. Then I have traced the story first of Nkore and then of the other former kingdoms, relying, as I have said, upon the traditional accounts which have been published, together with oral information which I have been given. The final chapters show how these kingdoms were brought under the direct rule of the Omugabe and incorporated in the administrative district of Ankole and how this district developed up to the year 1914. From 1890 onwards my principal source has been the records which exist in the Secretariat archives at Entebbe.

It may be wondered why I have chosen the year 1914 at which to stop this account. Events which are too close to the present day cannot be viewed with the perspective and detachment which a historian requires, and some date must be selected as a closing point. 1914 seems to me as good a date to choose as any, since in the first place it is the year in which, with the settlement of the Anglo-German frontier, Ankole attained the boundaries which she has today and which mark the final limit of her expansion westwards which had steadily progressed during the preceding centuries. Secondly, this was the year in which the First World War started, a war which was indirectly to have far-reaching consequences for Ankole as for the rest of the British Commonwealth and which was to produce as one of its results a new approach towards colonial administration.

The word Nkore is still used by Banyankore to signify the sazas of Nyabushozi, Kashari and Isingiro and part of Rwampara which formed the Omugabe's traditional kingdom

Chapter II

EARLY LEGENDS

IN the beginning, we are told, Ankole was an uninhabited country. Then Ruhanga, the Creator, came down from heaven to rule the land and, while in Ankole, three sons were born to him, Kakama, Kahima and Kairu. Wishing to discover which of his sons would be a worthy heir, he set them a test. Each was given a milkpot full of milk and told to keep it by him untouched throughout the night. At midnight Kakama spilt some of his milk but his two brothers filled up his pot again from theirs. Then, just before dawn, Kairu fell asleep and his pot upset and all his milk was lost. At dawn Ruhanga called his sons to him and, seeing how they had fared, decreed that Kairu should be the servant of his brothers for his milkpot was empty, that Kahima should be the herdsman of Kakama to whom he had given his milk and that Kakama should be the heir and ruler of the land. Then Ruhanga returned to heaven and Kakama, or Rugaba as he was also called, ruled as Omukama or Omugabe in his place. Rugaba was in turn succeeded by his son Nyamate and he by his son Ruyonga. None of these was an ordinary mortal for none suffered death but ascended into heaven at the end of his reign.

Ruyonga had his capital at Kishozi near Mubende and from there ruled over what is now Ankole and Buganda. There a daughter was born to him whom he called Nyamate after her grandfather. Ruyonga, wishing to make blood-brotherhood with Isaza the king of Kitara, sent messengers to him but Isaza deceived them and the ceremony was carried out with Bukuku, Isaza's gate-keeper, instead of the king. Ruyonga, when he discovered this, was very angry and, determined to get Isaza into his power, sent his daughter Nyamate to the king of Kitara. Isaza when he saw her was amazed at her beauty but Nyamate would not disclose who she was or whence she had come. Isaza, however, much as he loved her, loved his cattle more and when after a little while, being about to bear Isaza's child, she said she must return home, he made no attempt to prevent or to follow her. Eluding her companions whom Isaza had sent with her, she returned alone to her father. There she gave birth to a son, Isimbwa, the first Mucwezi.

Ruyonga, having failed to ensnare Isaza by means of his daughter, then chose two splendid beasts from his herds, the bull Ruhogo and the calf Kahogo, and his herdsman took them to Isaza's herds and left them

6

there. When Isaza saw the beasts he loved them greatly. Soon, however, they broke loose and made their way home and Isaza, when he found that they had gone, set out to follow them, leaving his gate-keeper, Bukuku, in charge in his absence. Weary in the pursuit of his beloved cattle, Isaza at last arrived at the palace of Ruyonga. There he was entertained by the king and there he found the beasts he sought and his wife and son. In Ruyonga's palace Isaza remained for the rest of his life and Bukuku ruled in Kitara in his place.[10]

Bukuku had a daughter, Nyinamwiru, whom the wise men advised him to kill for, they said, she would give birth to a prodigy who would cause his death. Bukuku, however, instead of killing her had her mutilated depriving her of one breast and one eye and had her kept in confinement. Now Isimbwa, the Mucwezi, who had inherited the kingdom of his grandfather Ruyonga, was hunting in Kitara when he came to the place where Nyinamwiru was confined. Making his way in, he spent several days with her and then departed. When in due course Nyinamwiru gave birth to Isimbwa's son and her father heard of it, he ordered the baby to be thrown into a nearby river. From there, however, the baby was rescued by a potter and brought up in secret in the potter's family. As the child, Ndahura, grew up he became known for his quarrelsome and overbearing manner and after a dispute with Bukuku's herdsman he came face to face with his grandfather and speared him, thus fulfilling the prophecy. Thereupon he was acknowledged as Nyinamwiru's son and acclaimed as king of Kitara. When Isimbwa saw that his son had established himself in Kitara, he handed over to him his kingdom also. These two kingdoms, however, were not enough for the warrior Ndahura who in a series of campaigns established the rule of the Bacwezi over an area covering almost the whole of what is now Uganda and the Lake Province of Tanganyika. Of the wonderful doings of the Bacwezi, the king Ndahura and his sons and relatives, both of their knowledge and their skill, there are many stories told and to them are attributed such monuments of the unknown past as the great earthworks at Bigo. Ndahura, however, met with disaster during one of his campaigns against Ihangiro and was captured. Although he was later rescued and returned to his capital near Mubende, he felt that, having once been a captive, he was no longer fit to rule and handed over the Bacwezi kingdom to his son Wamara. During Wamara's reign, a series of misfortunes befell the Bacwezi; their people became rebellious and the omens were persistently unfavourable. Finally, in disgust, they

---

10 According to the Bunyoro version of this tale, as told by Mrs. Fisher in *Twilight Tales of the Black Baganda*, Ruyonga (Nyamiyonga) was the king of the underworld and, in pursuit of the cattle, Isaza descended into hell where he was kept captive by its king.

decided to leave a land which had grown so ungrateful and Wamara with many of his followers, according to one account, disappeared into the lake in Singo which bears his name.

Wamara during the early years of his reign had had his capital at Itaba, a few miles from Mbarara,[11] and there a slave girl Njunaki had borne him a son, Ruhinda. When he had grown to manhood, Ruhinda had gone campaigning in Tanganyika and it was on his return that he found his father's capital, then at Ntusi in Bwera, deserted and the Bacwezi no longer in the land. His father's drum, Bagyendanwa, had been preserved for him by his maternal grandfather, Katuku, into whose care it had been given and taking this he was recognised as ruler of the southern part of the Bacwezi kingdom, that is to say the land south of the Rwizi river. The northern part of the kingdom fell to the Babiito Abakama of Bunyoro, whilst in the east the present dynasty of the Kabaka of Buganda was established.[12]   Later Ruhinda left the rule of the country between the Rwizi and Kagera rivers together with the drum Bagyendanwa to his son Nkuba and withdrew to his territories south of the Kagera where he died. In these southern lands in the present Lake Province of Tanganyika and in Urundi he left other sons who succeeded him as kings in their respective regions and throughout this area to this day the majority of ruling families look to Ruhinda as their ancestor.

---

11 In the present gombolola of Sabagabo Rwampara. The sacred grove which marks the site still exists, a landmark for miles around.

12 According to tradition the first Mubiito Omukama of Bunyoro, Rukidi, was a son of Kyomya, a half brother of Ndahura, born in Bukedi (the land north of the Nile) whilst Kato Kimera, who became Kabaka of Buganda, was his twin. It is now generally accepted that the Babiito are a dynasty of Nilotic origin.

Chapter III

NKORE

THE kingdom of Kaaro-Karungi (the beautiful land) as it was then called, which Nkuba ya Rurama the son of Ruhinda ruled, was at first restricted to a small region around his birthplace of Rurama[13] for to the north and east the areas of the Masha and Ngarama were in rebellion. Nkuba, however, attacked and defeated the rebellious chiefs, killing Murinda whose father had been placed in charge of the Masha by the Mucwezi Wamara. This brought Kaaro-Karungi's boundary to the Rwizi and for the next nine generations the kingdom was to consist roughly of the present county of Isingiro together with a small portion of Rwampara in the north-west. During this period the Abagabe usually had their capitals in the hills of the Kagarama area whilst nearby on the south-western shore of Lake Nakivali (Mazinga) lay the sacred forest of Ishanje to which the bodies of the Abagabe were carried on death and where, according to traditional rites, they were left to decompose for a certain period during which the land was in mourning and at the end of which it was claimed that the dead ruler had been reborn as a lion.

Nkuba's son Nyaika ruled in peace but in the reign of his son Nyabugaro (Ntare I) Nkore was subjected to a severe invasion by the Banyoro. The Babiito Abakama of Bunyoro claimed that as heirs of the Bacwezi they were the overlords of Kaaro-Karungi, the excellence of whose grazing lands and cattle were a tempting prey to her powerful neighbours who ruled north of the Rwizi. The Omukama Olimi I, having defeated the Baganda and slain their Kabaka Nakibingi, invaded Kaaro-Karungi, drove the Omugabe into exile and plundered the country. Frightened by an eclipse, so it is said, the Omukama withdrew;[14] but the country had been devastated. For several years cattle were so few in number that the Bahima were reduced to living on the fruits of the earth and men remember these years as Eijugo Nyonza, the time of the nyonza berries for bride price.

---

13 In the north of the present gombolola of Mutuba I Isingiro, about ten miles south-west of Gayaza.

14 The traditional account of the eclipse is poetically described in *Abagabe b'Ankole*, *op. cit.*, as follows: "the moon fell from the sky and plunged into the lake Mutukura and darkness covered the whole land and remained throughout noonday. Nyabugaro then brought cows and sheep for sacrifice and . . . when the sacrifice was over the moon lifted itself up and returned to its place in the sky."

Of the reigns of the succeeding Abagabe, Rushango and Kagwejegye-rera-Mishango (Ntare II), little is known. During the reign of the following Omugabe, Rugamba (Ntare III), it is said that a thunderbolt fell from the sky and where it fell it created Lake Mburo, causing widespread death to which was attributed the following evil of smallpox which then devas-tated the land. On the death of Rugamba's son, the Omugabe Kasasira, his two sons, Kitera and Rumongye, fought for the throne. This is the first account we have of a disputed succession but during the next two centuries it became customary for the death of an Omugabe to be immediately followed by a war of succession between his sons or brothers and it was often several years before the successful claimant to the throne could firmly establish himself. In this case the younger brother, Kitera, was at first successful and Rumongye had to take refuge in Karagwe. Rumongye, however, returned a few years later with a handful of followers and succeeded in defeating and killing his brother.

With the accession at the beginning of the eighteenth century of Ntare IV, Rumongye's grandson, Kaaro-Karungi entered a new phase in her history and during the succeeding two centuries a series of able and ener-getic Abagabe steadily extended her power northwards and westwards, mainly at the expense of Bunyoro and Mpororo. As a young man, Ntare visited in secret the kraal of Kamurari, the Omukama of Mpororo, and the Omukama, when he had discovered who he was, gave him two of his daughters, Kabibi and Mukabandi, as his wives. Previously, the Abagabe had always married into the Batwa and Baitira clans and, when Ntare returned with his Bashambo wives, he met with considerable opposition He was told that rain had fallen incessantly since he had gone to Mpororo and that the royal drums had been sounding on their own because of his marriage into a strange clan. As a result of this and of a later dynastic alliance made by his son, the greater part of Mpororo was to fall under the control of the Abagabe during the eighteenth century.

Early in his reign Ntare was attacked by Cwamali, Omukama of Bunyoro. Utterly defeated, Ntare fled for refuge first to the caves of Nyami-tsindo, then to Kantsyore island in the Kagera and finally to Muzira forest near Nsongezi. Even Bagyendanwa fell into the enemy's hands.[15]

Cwamali occupied the country for several years and then went on to conquer Ruanda. Here, however, the Banyoro over-reached themselves. Cwamali was defeated and killed and his army, retreating through Kaaro-Karungi, was set upon by Ntare and slaughtered, Ntare thus earning the

---

[15] On capturing Bagyendanwa, Cwamali ordered it to be cut open but, so it is said, the perpetrator of this sacrilege was struck down by lightning whilst blood flowed forth from the drum. Cwamali was so alarmed that he sent the drum back to Ntare.

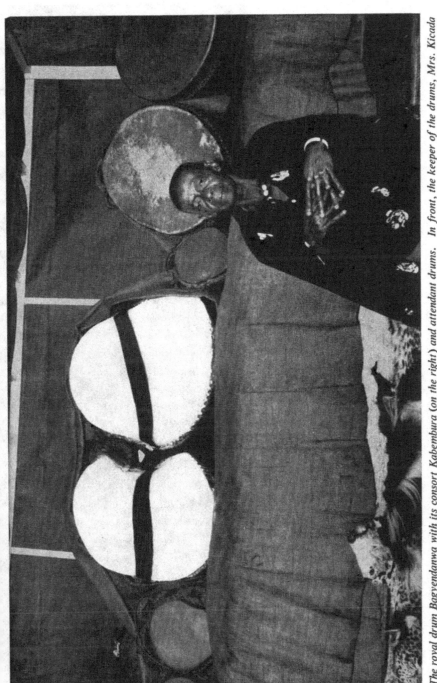

The royal drum Bagyendanwa with its consort Kabembura (on the right) and attendant drums. In front, the keeper of the drums, Mrs. Kicada of the Bararu clan.

Rubambansi Gasyonga II
Omugabe of Ankole

name of Kiitabanyoro. Cwamali's mother when she heard the news is said to have cried, "Ebi shi! Ente za Kaaro zankora omunda" (the cows of Kaaro have broken my heart). Thus did Kaaro get the name of Nkore.

The withdrawal of the Banyoro and the extension of the Omugabe's influence north of the Rwizi brought Ntare into conflict with the people of Buhweju and some mention of the struggle between the Omugabe's warriors, the Nyana, and the Omukama of Buhweju's warriors, the Nkondami, will be made in a later chapter. This struggle ended in a truce whereby Nkore gained control over a large part of Nyabushozi and part of Kashari.

Macwa, Ntare's son by his wife Mukabandi the Mpororo princess, is principally remembered for the expedition which he sent against Irebe, the Omukama of Bwera. This expedition is said to have returned with plunder consisting not only of cattle but also of Irebe's sacred circlet, Rutare, which was thereafter used by the Abagabe in the traditional rainmaking ceremonies. Macwa married his first cousin Nkazi, Kahaya Rutindangyezi of Mpororo's daughter, and their son was brought up at his maternal grandfather's court.

Macwa was succeeded by his son Rwabirere who, however, was struck down by a thunderbolt after reigning only a few months and the throne was seized by his brother Karara. His reign, however, was also short for he was soon after murdered by his brother Karaiga. Karaiga, fearing that Kahaya, another of his brothers, would try in his turn to supplant him, attempted to poison him. In this he was unsuccessful and Kahaya sent a force under his son Rwebishengye to attack the usurper. Karaiga was defeated and fled to Buganda where later he died and Kahaya became Omugabe.

Nkore at this time greatly extended her boundaries westward, for Kahaya was the heir of his maternal grandfather, Kahaya of Mpororo, a large part of whose kingdom including Shema and much of Rwampara he inherited. Furthermore, according to tradition, Kahaya was the first Omugabe to carry out the ceremony of bathing in the pool Kijongo which lies a few miles from the present trading centre of Ibanda.[16] If tradition is correct in this, then the Omugabe's kingdom at this time must have extended almost as far north as the Katonga river. The Banyoro were never to recover their influence in these parts and the eighteenth century saw the steady decline of that kingdom until, by its close, the loss of Buddu and the defection of Koki left nothing of Bunyoro rule south of the Katonga. But if Nkore was no longer to stand in fear of her old enemy

---

16 Each of Kahaya's successors until Mutambuka is said to have undergone this ritual bathe as part of his coronation ceremonies.

to the north, her expansion westwards was to bring her into contact with a new rival, Ruanda, and during Kahaya's reign an invading army under the Umwami Kigyere III penetrated into Shema before it was driven out.

Kahaya's death was followed by civil war between his sons. Nyakashaija, having been installed as Omugabe, attacked and defeated his elder brother Rwebishengye. The latter, however, sought aid from the Kabaka Kamanya and entered Nkore with a Baganda army. Nyakashaija fled but Rwebishengye merely returned to Buganda with plunder. From there he sent another force under his brother Bwarenga against Nyakashaija who this time was defeated, captured and put to death. Bwarenga, however, instead of handing over the kingdom to his brother, was himself installed as Omugabe and it was not until his death a short while later that Rwebishengye inherited his father's kingdom.

Rwebishengye carried on the work of expansion which his father, grandfather and great-grandfather had started. In the west he invaded and plundered Buhweju and in the east he wrested Kabula from the Banyoro. On his northern boundary he appointed the famous witch Murogo to act as spy on the Banyoro north of the Katonga. Murogo and her female descendants were reputed to be able to turn themselves into cattle and then to mix with the herds of the enemy and to hear their secrets. They served the Abagabe for several generations in the Ibanda area and the last of them, Julia Kibubura, was to become the only female gombolola chief to be appointed by the British Administration.

During the last few years of Rwebishengye's reign strife broke out among the princes who rebelled against their father and on the Omugabe's death Kayungu set himself up as ruler and fought his elder brother Gasyonga. Although, after several years of fighting, Gasyonga was victorious, he had scarcely established himself as Omugabe when Bagyendanwa was seized by his uncle Rwanga and it was several more years before Gasyonga succeeded in supplanting him. Gasyonga is remembered as a peaceable and benevolent ruler who during his reign suffered three invasions from the Baganda whose Kabaka was at that time Suna II. Gasyonga's son Mutambuka, on the other hand, was a warrior king and in his reign Nkore once again waged aggressive campaigns against her neighbours. Expeditions were sent against the rulers of Igara and Buhweju to assert the rights of the Omugabe as their overlord and Toro, Busongora and Karagwe were invaded and plundered. It was during his Busongora campaign that Mutambuka captured and then married the Mubiito princess Kiboga who was later, when her son Ntare had come to the throne, to have a deciding influence on the policies of Nkore. The Omukama of Koki, Isansa, so it is said, was rash enough to make uncomplimentary remarks about

Mutambuka's personal appearance and a force was sent into Isansa's kingdom and slew him. This so angered Isansa's overlord, the Kabaka Mutesa, that he in his turn invaded Nkore.

Mutambuka died in about the year 1870 and there was the customary scramble for power among the princes. Mukwenda was proclaimed Omugabe but his brother Rukongye with a considerable body of followers defied him. When Rukongye had been defeated and killed, his supporters, having given their allegiance to another brother Makumbi, fled to Kabula. The youngest of Mukwenda's brothers, Ntare, who was not as yet a serious rival on account of his youth and of the fact that he was the son of a captive, although of the royal clan of Bunyoro, fearing his brother's intentions joined Makumbi's force in Kabula. Mukwenda appealed for help to Mutesa of Buganda who sent his Pokino Mukasa into Kabula. Mukasa, by an offer of blood-brotherhood and of help against Mukwenda, enticed seventy of the leaders of Makumbi's force, including twenty of the royal clan, to meet him and thereupon had them massacred. Ntare who had had the good fortune not to be one of the seventy, was then accepted as the leader of the anti-Mukwenda party and his pretensions to the throne were supported by the claim that Mutambuka had before his death named him as his successor and by a prophecy that the son of a foreigner should rule Nkore. Fleeing west with the surviving members of his force, Ntare was attacked and defeated by Mukwenda. He eluded his pursuers, however, and though later given poison by an agent of Mukwenda, he continued, with the support of his indomitable mother Kiboga, to defy his brother who once again called upon Buganda for help. Still suffering from the effects of the poison he had been given and also stricken with smallpox, Ntare took refuge in Buhweju. From there he moved with his followers into Mitoma where at Mugoye the longest and most bitter of the wars of succession came to an end when, after a battle lasting three days, Mukwenda's army was defeated and he himself slain on the battlefield.

Ntare, like his father, is remembered as one of the great warrior Abagabe. During his reign the Omugabe's power reached its furthest extent. Not only did the neighbouring kingdoms of Buhweju, Igara and Buzimba recognise Ntare as their overlord, but further afield the rulers of Kitagwenda and Bwera would send him presents to avert invasion whilst raiding parties for plunder were sent into Rujumbura and Ruanda. The boundary with Buganda is said to have lain as far to the east as the Kyogya river.

Ntare had, however, to contend with the growing power of Buganda which, with the conquest of Buddu at the end of the preceding century, had been Nkore's eastern neighbour and which had, as has already been seen during the last two reigns, raided Nkore and taken part in her civil

wars. During the latter years of Mutesa's reign, moreover, raiding parties
were sent three times into Nkore and returned with plunder. In 1888
the Baganda Christians, fleeing from persecution, asked Ntare for help.
Kiboga, remembering all that her son had suffered at the hands of the
Baganda, advised him to kill them, but Ntare allowed them to settle in
Kabula. Ungrateful guests, the Baganda were later to take that country
from Nkore.

In Ntare's reign Nkore made her first contact with the colonising
powers of Europe which, during the eighteen-eighties and nineties, were to
establish their spheres of influence over the hitherto secluded tribes and
kingdoms of East Africa and which were in a short time radically to alter
the traditional structure and mode of life of these people. In 1852, in
Mutambuka's reign, the Arab Snay bin Amir, the first adventurer from the
outside world to enter Nkore, passed through the kingdom on his way to
Buganda from where he returned south to bring news of what he had seen
to the explorer Burton. In 1889 H. M. Stanley, returning from the relief
of Emin Pasha, passed through Buzimba, Buhweju and Nkore. Messages
of friendship were exchanged between Stanley and Ntare and at Byaruha,
some fifteen miles south of Mbarara, Stanley and Bucunku, Ntare's representative and first cousin, made blood-brotherhood. Stanley apparently
understood this ceremony as being in fact a treaty whereby the Omugabe
had handed over to him sovereignty over his kingdom and in 1890 Stanley
produced to the Imperial British East Africa Company the following
document:

"This is to certify that we, Uchunku, Prince of Ankori and Mpororo, by authority
and on behalf of my father, Antari, the King and the chiefs and elders of the tribe of
Wanyankori, occupying and owning the territory of Ankori and Mpororo, do hereby
cede to Bula Matari (or H. M. Stanley), our friend, all rights of government of the said
districts, and we hereby grant him or his representative the sovereign right and right of
government over our country for ever, and in consideration of value received, and the
protection he has accorded us and our neighbours against Kabba Rega and his son
Warasura; and in token thereof we endow him with the spear of Antari, and his son, the
heir of his power.

"In witness whereof we have declared in this moon (May 1888[17]) that we have made
this gift to him, in the presence of our people and his white companions; and we call
upon all concerned to observe the rights of Bula Matari (or H. M. Stanley), his representatives or assigns.

(signed) THOS. HEAZLE PARKE, Surgeon, Army Medical Staff.
A. J. MOUNTENEY JEPHSON.
ROBT. HENRY NELSON.
W. G. STAIRS, Lieutenant, R.E."

The rights which Stanley believed he possessed under this and other
similar "treaties" of concession, he voluntarily transferred to the Imperial
British East Africa Company. Before, however, any attempt was made
by the Company to test the validity of such a document, Captain F. D.
Lugard had, in 1891, entered into fresh negotiations with the Omugabe.

---

[17] The blood-brotherhood ceremony was, in fact, carried out on the 22nd July, 1889.

In 1890 Jackson had on behalf of the Imperial British East Africa Company entered into negotiations with the Kabaka Mwanga. The boundary between the British and the German spheres of influence had not at that time been defined as far west as Uganda, and Germany, who was extending her influence over what is now Tanganyika, was keen to get a foothold also in Uganda. In July of that year, however, an agreement was made between Great Britain and Germany whereby the former, in return for surrendering her sovereignty over Heligoland off the German coast, obtained within her sphere of influence the territory north of the parallel of latitude 1° south. This placed almost the whole of the present Uganda Protectorate within the British sphere. In the following December Lugard persuaded Mwanga to enter into a formal treaty recognising the suzerainty of the Imperial British East Africa Company which in turn undertook the protection of his kingdom and the provision of a Resident and officials to assist in its administration. This treaty applied only to the Kabaka's kingdom but the Kabaka maintained that the kingdoms of the west together with other states such as Busoga and Kiziba had for generations paid him tribute. Lugard was not prepared to enforce these claims, the validity of which was in any case doubtful. He was, however, aware of the advantages of extending the Company's influence over the area to the west of Buganda. Kabarega of Bunyoro was in league with the Muslims in rebellion against Mwanga and Nkore, bordering on the German sphere of influence south of the Kagera, lay in a strategic position since it controlled the main route whereby Kabarega obtained arms from the German sphere. In June 1891 Lugard entered Nkore from Buddu bringing with him Kasagama who had been driven out of Toro by Kabarega and whom Lugard proposed to reinstate. The purpose of Lugard's journey was to reach Lake Albert and obtain the support of the Sudanese troops left there by Emin Pasha and on the way to enter into treaties with Nkore and Toro. At Nyabushozi, he met the Omugabe's envoys; the ceremony of blood-brotherhood was again carried out; and a treaty was made whereby Ntare accepted the protection of the Imperial British East Africa Company and undertook not to allow the passage of arms through his kingdom.[18] No administrative post was set up and indeed the Company was in no position to take on fresh commitments, complete withdrawal from Uganda being seriously proposed at the end of 1891. No withdrawal was made, however, though it was constantly threatened during the following years and in 1893 the British Government took over from the Imperial British East Africa Company all responsibilities as the protecting power in Buganda.[19]

---

[18] For the text of the treaty see the Appendix.
[19] The British protectorate over Buganda was formally established in June 1894.

In 1893 a party of Germans under Major Langheld passed through Nkore and Ntare, alarmed by this, appealed for the protection promised by Lugard's treaty. In July 1894 the Commissioner accordingly instructed Major G. G. Cunningham to try to make a new treaty, stating: "You will render him (Ntare) any assistance in your power against the Ruanda or other tribes in the habit of raiding into his territory, but will on no account cross the German frontier. You will ascertain how far Ntali has any cause of complaint against the Ruanda in order that I may represent the matter to the German officials. I am anxious to establish a station in Ankoli for the purpose of stopping illicit trade (i.e. in arms or slaves)." Cunningham had some difficulty in getting Ntare's agreement to the treaty for the Omugabe had apparently had second thoughts on the desirability of calling in the British, and procrastinated. Eventually, the Enganzi Mbaguta came to Cunningham and signed the treaty on Ntare's behalf, Cunningham signing on behalf of the Queen (29 August, 1894). In a letter to the Commissioner, Cunningham writes: "The Katikiro Magota arrived with full powers (he said).   He signed the treaty for the King, requested that a black man might be sent in future as your representative as Ntali could not see a European. He said that the king did not wish for a post in Ankoli at present." The treaty provided that there should be peace between the British and the Banyankore; that British subjects should have free access to all parts of Ntare's kingdom and should have the right to possess property and to trade there; and that Ntare would not cede any territory to, or enter into any treaty with, any foreign power without consent.[20]

The last years of Ntare's reign were unhappy ones. Rinderpest had decimated the cattle and smallpox was rampant, Ntare losing his son Kabumbire from the disease. Finally, the Banyaruanda, provoked by the successful Banyankore raids of a few years before, invaded the country. Before the Banyaruanda had been driven out of Nkore, Ntare had died of pneumonia in the year 1895. With the death of Ntare V, the period of Nkore's history which had started with the reign of his namesake, Ntare Kiitabanyoro, came to an end.

---

[20] For the text of the treaty see the Appendix.

Chapter IV

MPORORO

THE kingdom of Mpororo which, for the short period of its independent existence, comprised south-west Ankole, part of Ruanda and most of Kigezi suddenly made its appearance during the seventeenth century and as suddenly disintegrated. Traditional accounts, which are few, allow for two Abakama only, Kamurari and Kahaya, and some do not even recognise the former as an actual Omukama. Tradition does not satisfactorily explain whence these rulers of Mpororo came. They and their fellow Bashambo, the main clan to which all the leading Mpororo sub-clans belong, appear to have come into the county from the south or south-west. They were, it seems, the last of the periodic waves of Hamitic people to enter Ankole, the Bahima of Ankole proper, with whom they are almost identical in appearance and language, having preceded them by several centuries. There are, however, important differences between the traditions of Mpororo and those of the other kingdoms of the Western Province of Uganda and the Lake Province of Tanganyika. In all the latter kingdoms the Bacwezi have in the past been worshipped and the rulers claim descent from them. The traditions of the Bahororo, however, are in many ways associated more with Ruanda than with the rest of Uganda and it is the goddess Nyabingi, rather than the Bacwezi, in whom the people stand in awe.

Most of the Bashambo clans have no traditions concerning any ancestors of Kamurari, the founder of Mpororo. The head of the Beenerugambagye, on the other hand, gives the names of six of these ancestors all of whom are said to have lived in Mpororo. The first was called Muntu, and from him descended Kazi, Karagaire, Muzora, Ntagu, Kinwa and Kamurari. Traditional accounts are fairly consistent in agreeing that Kamurari and his brother Ishemurari entered what is now the Ankole saza of Kajara where they found the Amazon Queen Kitami whose subjects were all women. From Kitami, whose death is ascribed to the sting of a bee and whose spirit was later worshipped as Nyabingi, Kamurari procured the drum Murorwa and control of the neighbouring country. He took for his wife Mikyera of the Beeneishekatwa clan which he found in Kajara, and near Rwentobo can still be seen the bark-cloth tree which is said to mark the site of the birth of their son Kahaya Rutindangyezi.

17

*Areas ruled by Bashambo clans in the
second half of the nineteenth century*

Under Kahaya, Mpororo extended its frontiers to include all Kigezi (except the modern Bufumbira saza and part of Kinkizi), the Ankole sazas of Kajara, Igara, Shema and Rwampara (except the low ground south of the Rwizi river) and the northern portion of Ruanda. Kahaya had a large family, from whom the important sub-clans of the Bashambo trace their origin, and its members established themselves in various parts of his kingdom. One son only, Mafundo, whose mother was a slave girl, was given a drum and the authority that went with it. His territory was the important kingdom of Igara which lay across the salt route to Lakes Edward and George. Many Bahororo claim that Ruanda proper also was subordinate to Kahaya who is said to have established the present dynasty[21] on the throne. It is stated that Kahaya gave Ruanda to his brother Kirima whose son he undertook to bring up with his own family. While the boy was in Mpororo, Kahaya by mistake lamed him by treading on his foot. Then, nicknaming him "Kigyere" (*omugyere* a foot), he sent him back to his father with the promise that he would always support him against his enemies. There seems, however, to be nothing in Ruanda tradition to support the idea of the subordination of that country to Mpororo. The Batutsi of Ruanda, though similar to the Bahororo, are not the same people and have a different language. Furthermore, the pedigree of the Ruanda Abaami, which gives twenty generations prior to Kirima father of Kigyere, makes no mention of Kamurari, though, on the other hand, the second and third Abakama have the names of Muntu and Kazi, which correspond to those in the Beenerugambagye pedigree.

In Kahaya's reign close relations were established with the neighbouring kingdom of Nkore as the result first of the marriage between the Omugabe Ntare Kiitabanyoro and Kamurari's daughters and then of the marriage between the Omugabe Macwa and his first cousin Nkazi, Kahaya's daughter. Since that time it has been customary for Abagabe to choose Bashambo wives.

Kahaya Rutindangyezi had seven sons, all of whom were disobedient to their father. Kahaya therefore disinherited them and buried the drum Murorwa so that none of them should succeed him, making his grandson by his daughter Nkazi, the Omugabe Kahaya I, whom he had brought up, his heir. Though some portions of Mpororo continued to maintain an independent or semi-independent position under the descendants of Kahaya's sons who established themselves in various parts of Mpororo, the kingdom in general from then on accepted either the Omugabe of Nkore or the Umwami of Ruanda as overlord.

Deposed 1961.

THE DESCENDANTS OF KAHAYA RUTINDANGYEZI

SHOWING THE PRINCIPAL BASHAMBO SUB-CLANS WHICH THEY FOUNDED AND THE PRESENT ADMINISTRATIVE UNITS WHICH ROUGHLY CORRESPOND TO THE AREAS WHICH THEY WERE RULING TOWARDS THE END OF THE NINETEENTH CENTURY.

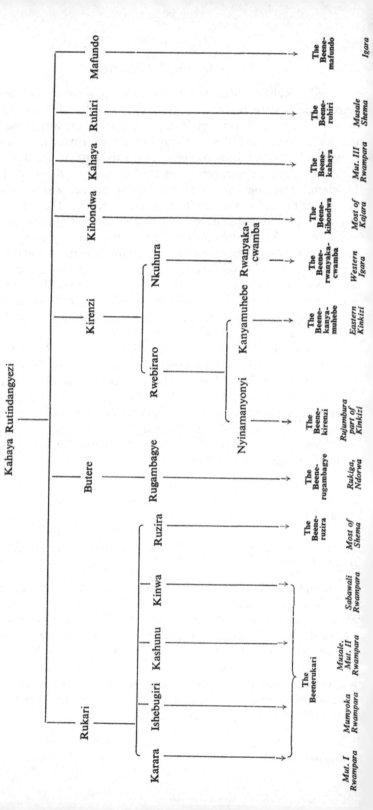

Igara, though in the Omugabe's sphere of influence, retained its independence until the middle of the nineteenth century when the over-rule of the Omugabe was established. Its rulers, the Beenemafundo, had their drum, Kihoza, and maintained the ceremonies normally associated with full Abakama.[22] Of the two successors of Mafundo, Kinwa and Rwihura, little is known, but the third Omukama, Kajuga, is remembered as a tyrant who tortured his subjects and seized their cattle. It is said that the name Igara was given to the county in his reign on account of the number of people who had been blinded by their king, the verb *okwigara* meaning to stop up or blind. After the death of Kajuga's son, Katana, Igara came under the over-rule of Nkore. The Banyankore helped Namarenga to drive out his cousin Rutondo, Katana's son, and later, when he showed signs of rebellion, he was deposed and Rutondo brought back. Rutondo's son Musinga was Omukama when the British administration was established.

Shema came very early under the Omugabe's rule. It is said by some that it was given by Kamurari as a wedding present when Ntare married Mukabandi. Others say that Kahaya Rutindangyezi gave it to the Omugabe when his grandson Ruzira married Bunyonyo, daughter of the Omugabe Macwa. The dominant clan in the greater part of the present saza was the Beeneruzira who had given a port on round Kyangyenyi Hill to the Beeneishemurari, a clan descended form Kamurari's brother Ishemurari which had been driven out of Kajara by the Beenekihondwa. In the west of the saza, however, a Bashambo clan, the Beenemuganga, had established themselves and were a periodic source of trouble to the Abagabe.[23]

Rwampara was also subordinate to the Abagabe. Most of this saza was under the control of the Beenerukari who had, however, split up into various sub-clans each with its own area.

The dominant clan in Kajara, which was within the orbit of Ruanda, was the Beenekihondwa. Most of the present gombolola of Sabadu, however, formed, with part of Ruanda, the area of Butaya and was ruled by the Bagina, descendants of Kagina, son-in-law of Kahaya Rutindangyezi. The Anglo-German boundary cut this area in half.

The present district of Kigezi was divided between the Beenekirenzi in Rujumbura and Kinkizi and the Beenerugambagye in Ndorwa and Rukiga. Towards the end of the nineteenth century, however, the expansion of the Bakiga resulted in the Beenerugambagye being driven out of their ancestral home. The parts of Mpororo now comprised in Kigezi

---

22 The drums and other regalia still survive in a good state of preservation and are kept by the grandson of the last Omukama in the gombola of Sabadu Igara

23 The last of the Beenemaganga rulers, Bwesharire, rebelled against his overlord Ntare V and was defeated and captured by Ntare's nephew Igumira. While in captivity he committed suicide by setting the house he was in on fire.

were from time to time subject to raids from Ruanda but, it would seem, never had any dealings with the Omugabe. At the beginning of the present century, however, the Omugabe attempted, as heir of Mpororo, to assert his authority over Rujumbura but, as will be seen later, without success.

Chapter V

BUHWEJU

BUHWEJU, it is said, was the domain of Nyinamwiru, the daughter of Bukuku and the mother of the Mucwezi Ndahura. Its ruler under Nyinamwiru's suzerainty was Muramira, a man of great knowledge who constructed a tunnel which came out at the foot of the Buhweju hills and by means of which he could escape from his enemies.

At this time there were in Mpororo, in the present Ankole saza of Kajara, three poor Bahima brothers of the Bariisa clan. A mystic eagle which flashed like lightning built its nest in the brothers' house and, on consulting a sorcerer, they were told that, if they followed the eagle, they would make their fortune. The eagle, when it had hatched and fledged its young, flew northwards and the brothers Kataizi, Rugo and Kinyonyi, accompanied by their sister Iremera, followed it. Each night it would alight upon a tree and the four would sleep beneath the branches. When they reached Buhweju, Kataizi, worn out by the journey, would go no further. His descendants became cultivators or Bairu and the Bataizi clan remains in Buhweju today. The others continued their journey and finally the eagle led them to the court of Ndahura in whose service they enlisted. Ndahura having fallen in love with Iremera married her,[24] and to his brothers-in-law, Kinyonyi and Rugo, he presented the kingdoms of Buhweju and Buzimba. First, however, Muramira had to be disposed of. In this Kinyonyi was aided by one of Muramira's chiefs who, taking revenge upon his master who had seduced his sister, betrayed the secret of the tunnel, and as Muramira emerged from it he was set upon and killed by Kinyonyi's men who lay in wait for him. In this way did Kinyonyi, with the drum Mashaija which Ndahura had given him, become Omukama of Buhweju and establish the Bariisa dynasty which ruled until the beginning of the present century.

The traditional genealogy of the Bariisa Abakama, from Kinyonyi to Ndagara who was killed in 1901, allows for only fifteen Abakama and fourteen generations. Yet over the same period of time, that is from the end of the Bacwezi dynasty, the Banyankore account for seventeen generations

---

[24] Iremera, a Muriisa wife of Ndahura, also figures in Bunyoro tradition in which it is stated that Rukidi the first Mubiito Omukama when he entered Kitara after the departure of the Bacwezi found Iremera and other wives of the Bacwezi and married them. It is said to have been Iremera who taught Rukidi to like milk and to follow the customs of the cattle people. She was the mother of the twins Ocaki and Oyo, Rukidi's successors.

of Abagabe and the Banyoro for seventeen generations of Abakama. The Buzimba genealogy has been even further telescoped and records only seven generations from Rugo to Nduru the last Omukama. Kinyonyi's successors, though subordinate to the Abakama of Bunyoro the heirs of the Bacwezi and later to the Abagabe of Nkore, had all the ceremonies and regalia of an independent kingdom and the royal drum Mashaija with its attendant drums and *nkondo* (crowns with colobus monkey beards) still survive.

Of the successors of Kinyonyi, Kabundami I, Kashoma I, Mugimba I, Karamagi I, Kashoma II and Mugimba II, little is known except the manner of their death. When the Omukama of Bunyoro died the Omukama of Buhweju would be sent for and, decked in ceremonial beads, would be led to execution by beheading.

In the reign of Mugimba II's son, Kabundami II, probably at the turn of the seventeenth century, the tyranny of Bunyoro was broken. Kabundami, who was determined that he would not suffer the fate of his fathers, gathered together a band of warriors known as the Nkondami. The leader of this band, a prince of the royal house, was known as Muguta ya Butaho Enshungyera Nigacweka owa Kinika kya Katago Rubabirira Omunyanshambo ou Engabo ye Ekira Ezindi.[25] When the messengers came from the Omukama of Bunyoro to lead Kabundami off to execution, Muguta took his place and, dressed in his master's execution robes, was escorted together with his followers to Bunyoro. Here they were bound and an axe placed before each of them. But Muguta's page began to recite his praises and Muguta, leaping into the air, was carried into the clouds, whereupon the sky roared and the Nkondami, overpowering their captors, beheaded them with their own axes. Then they caught and bound the Omukama of Bunyoro himself who, crying for mercy, promised that thenceforth the axe would be used to cut down trees and not men.

The defeat of the Banyoro by Ntare IV of Nkore gave Muguta his opportunity to occupy Kashari and to conquer Nshara. Stories of the heroism of Muguta and his Nkondami are still recited. As in all stories of Bahima warriors, cattle is the favourite theme and the best-known story is probably that of the Omukama of Buhweju's cow Mayenje ga Ishinjo Rutanyobwa Bigomba. This wonderful cow which gave daily six pots of milk was coveted by Ntare of Nkore. The latter, therefore, sent two famous thieves, Rucu Rwa Bugoro and Runkunku, to bring him the cow. By various deceits, the two thieves managed to get hold of the cow and, having disguised its colour by means of chalk and soot, brought it to their

---

[25] Muguta the son of Butaho who leaps in the air when spears are breaking, of Kinika Kya Katago, the speedy one, who inflicts deadly injuries, whose shield excels all others.

master. This led to war between the Nkondami and the Omugabe's warriors the Nyana under their leader Ntsinga. After various encounters during which Muguta and Ntsinga displayed feats of bravery, peace was made whereby Mayenje ga Ishinjo was returned to its owner and a boundary between Nkore and Buhweju agreed upon which divided Kashari between the two kingdoms and left Nshara and most of Nyabushozi in the hands of the Omugabe. Stories tell of the exploits of Muguta far afield. He and his Nkondami are said to have penetrated to Bukedi and it is near the site of Jinja that he is said to have been fatally injured. Falling from a tree, he was pierced by a stake and disembowelled. Concealing his injuries from his followers, he returned home holding in place his rotting entrails. Entering in before his king, he expired at his feet.

After the death of Muguta, the lands he had won east of the Buhweju escarpment fell to the Abagabe who, extending their domain over the whole of Kashari, Nyabushozi and Mitoma, succeeded Bunyoro as the overlords of Buhweju. There is little to be told of the Abakama who followed, Kashoma III, known as Gatukwire (the red-eyed), who had been one of Muguta's Nkondami, Kabundami III and Karamagi II.

Karamagi II left two sons Rukumba and Rusharabaga. The latter was intended by his father to be his heir but Rukumba, relying on Nkore support, for he and the Omugabe Kahaya I had married sisters, seized the throne. Then they took their case to Kahaya to judge but Rukumba, not content with this, tried to spear Rusharabaga who had to flee to the drum Bagyendanwa for refuge before escaping to Ruanda. Later, returning to Buhweju, he attacked his brother's palace at Rukiri and, having defeated him, became Omukama in his place. During his reign Buhweju was invaded by the Omugabe Rwebishengye, Kahaya's son.

Rusharabaga was succeeded by his son Kashoma IV and he by his son Ndagara. Born about 1820, Ndagara had an eventful life. Early in his reign he invaded Toro and took much plunder. Then Mutambuka, Rwebishengye's grandson, invaded Buhweju and devastated the country. For four years Ndagara fought against the Banyankore until, finally, he fled, first to Mpororo and then to Ruanda. On the death of Mutambuka he returned to Buhweju. During the civil war which followed Mutambuka's death, Ntare fled to Buhweju suffering from poison given him by his page at the instigation of his brother Mukwenda. He asked Ndagara for help and the latter consulted the oracles to see whether the future lay with Mukwenda or Ntare. The answer being favourable to Ntare, an antidote had to be found for the poison from which Ntare was suffering. This was to be a mixture with beer, but the country had been so ravaged by Mutambuka that messengers had to go to Kitagwenda to get the beer. Ntare

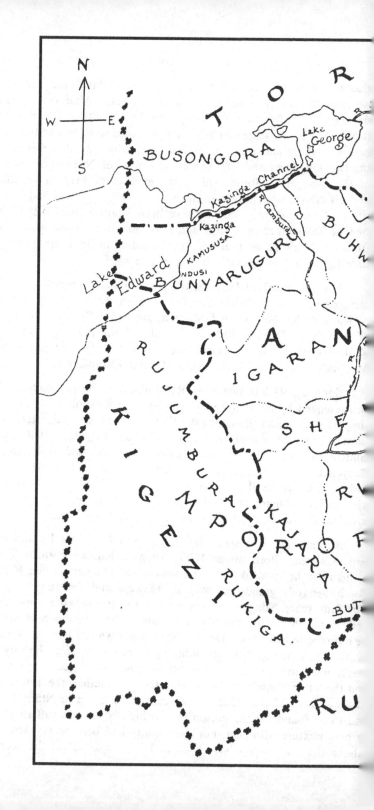

Map of ANKOLE District —
Showing the principal places mentioned in the text.

recovered but Mukwenda sent an army in pursuit and he had to flee from Buhweju. Ndagara, however, continued to support him and when the civil war was finally decided at Mugoye, Nyakiga, Ndagara's son was fighting in Ntare's army. Ndagara remained the friend of Ntare throughout the Omugabe's reign and men from Buhweju accompanied him on his campaigns against Busongora, Igara, Toro, Rujumbura and Ruanda.

Chapter VI

BUZIMBA

THE story of how the two brothers, Rugo and Kinyonyi, followed the mystic eagle to the court of Ndahura has been told in the last chapter. To Rugo, Ndahura gave the kingdom of Buzimba. Some Banyabuhweju, however, maintain that Buzimba was at first included in Kinyonyi's kingdom, but that when Kinyonyi found that the area was too large for him to rule effectively Ndahura sent Rugo to help him. The Banyabuzimba, on the other hand, deny that Buzimba was ever subordinate to Buhweju.

Practically no traditional accounts survive of the subsequent history of Buzimba. The names of only seven Abakama are remembered: Rugo, Kantu, Mukindo, Nyaruyonga, Mugarura, Nyakairu and Nduru.[26] These Abakama, like those of Buhweju, possessed regalia such as is found in neighbouring and more important kingdoms. The drum Bitunta, which Ndahura is said to have given to Rugo, is of particular interest on account of its minute size: it is little more than three inches high and is covered with the skin of the monitor lizard.

First subordinate to Bunyoro, Buzimba came under the control of Nkore in the reign of the Omugabe Rwebishengye. Ntare ya Kiboga, during the civil war with his brother Mukwenda, attacked Nyakairu of Buzimba, plundering 600 of his cattle and wounding his son Nduru. Nyakairu, with his family and his brother, another Rugo, fled to Bunyoro and there he died. During Kabarega's wars, Nduru, Nyakairu's son, decided to return with his seventy head of cattle. On the way, however, he was attacked by Nubian soldiers who took all he possessed. Destitute, he arrived at Ntare's kraal at Muti within the present township of Mbarara, and submitted to the Omugabe. On payment of one cow, which he procured from a friend, he was in 1894 restored by Ntare to his kingdom which he continued to rule as the Omugabe's vassal until the coming of the British.

---

26 Gorju in *Entre le Victoria, l'Albert et l'Edouard* also refers to six successors of Rugo but he states that their names alternated between that of Mukindo and that of Mugarura, the last Mukindo being also known as Nduru.

Chapter VII

BUNYARUGURU

THE Banyampaka who ruled this area were a Bahororo clan which is said to have come from Rujumbura and to have settled, first near Katwe and then at Kasenyi on Lake George, under the over-rule of the Babiito Abakama of Busongora, who themselves owed allegiance to the Abakama of Bunyoro. With the valuable salt deposits around Kasenyi under their control, this Hamitic clan succeeded in the nineteenth century in establishing its rule over a wide area comprising the much-prized grazing land on the southern and eastern shores of Lake George and on the south bank of the Kazinga channel. This chieftainship is said to have extended south of the channel, from Lake Edward to the Mpanga river, and to have included the high ground of Bunyaruguru proper.

Although these Banyampaka chiefs can hardly be dignified with the title of Abakama, they once possessed, so it is said, a drum, Mugonzi, now no longer in existence. The names of six rulers are remembered: Nkomyo, Ihungo, Goro, Rutairuka, Kasheshe and Kuri-ofire.

Towards the end of the eighteenth century, a group of Baganda, known as the Bakunta, murdered the Kabaka Junju at the instigation of his twin brother Semakokiro. Fleeing from the vengeance of the ungrateful Semakokiro, they travelled westward and a portion of them settled in Bunyaruguru. They are said to have introduced into that fertile area the banana and the bark-cloth tree, and their descendants, together with those of Bakonjo settlers of the next century, form the majority of the mixed population, with its distinctive dialect, which is found today in Bunyaruguru saza.

In about the year 1890, when Kabarega's army had overrun Busongora, Kaihura, a nephew of Bwacari the last Omukama of Busongora, fled from the Banyoro across the Kazinga channel. In return for a present of seven head of cattle, Arari, one of Kuri-ofire's chiefs, allowed him to settle near the present fishing village of Kazinga. Kaihura was not, however, content to remain an obscure exile. His cousin Kiboga was the mother of the Omugabe and he offered to conquer and hold the whole of Kuri-ofire's territory as one of Ntare's chiefs. To this Ntare agreed and, with the help of the Banyankore, Kaihura made himself chief of the land below the Bunyaruguru escarpment which lay between Lake Edward and the Cambura river.

Meanwhile, Lugard had reinstated Kasagama as Omukama of Toro and both Busongora and Kuri-otire's country north of the Kazinga were included in his kingdom. Kuri-ofire objected, but without avail. William Grant, writing in 1893, says: "There is a chief called Kuriafiri on an island in the lake who refuses to recognise Kasagama as Sultan. I told him he would have to do so. Mr. Reddie, I understand, made him a free Sultan but as the country was given to Kuriafiri by Kasagama's people I think it is but right that he should recognise Kasagama as Sultan." Kuri-ofire's country north of the Kazinga channel was formally incorporated in Toro by an appendix to the treaty of 3 March, 1894, between Major Owen and Kasagama; and Kuri-ofire withdrew south of the channel where he managed to maintain his independence of both Kasagama and Ntare in the high land of Bunyaruguru proper and east of the Cambura until 1900.[27]

According to an official report made in 1900, there were at that time four chieftainships in what is now Bunyaruguru saza: Kazinga ruled by Kaihura; Bunyarugur ruled by Kuri-ofire; Ndusi ruled by Katuramu; and Kamususa ruled by Byasigwa.

Chapter VIII
THE CREATION OF ANKOLE DISTRICT

WHEN the Omugabe Ntare died in 1895, there was no obvious neir to succeed him. His nephew, Kahitsi, seized Bagyendanwa and the royal herds but was unable to secure the support of the majority of the Bahima, who looked to the warrior Igumira, another of Ntare's nephews, as their leader. Igumira brought forward a youth, Kahaya, who, he claimed, was the son of Ntare and the rightful Omugabe. Matters were further complicated when Manyatsi, a cousin of Ntare who had quarrelled with Igumira and left Ankole for Baganda, asserted the claim of a third Muhinda, a boy Rwakatogoro, the son of Nkuranga, a popular prince whom Ntare, his brother, had murdered in a fit of suspicion.[28]

Kahitsi, unable to secure the throne unaided, made common cause with Igumira against Rwakatogoro and appealed to the Protectorate Government and to the Kabaka of Buganda for support. George Wilson, the Sub-Commissioner of Buganda, writing to the Commissioner in December 1895, states as follows:

"On July 31st, Kampala messengers to Ankole returned with definite news of the death of Mtali (Ntare) about the middle of that month. Ankole was in a disturbed condition. Further messengers were sent to the borders to gather information. These returned early in October, reporting that several claimants had endeavoured to take advantage of the state of anarchy brought about by Mtali's death: but these had been reduced to two boys: one produced by Kaish (Kahitsi) and Gomira (Igumira), two of the strongest brothers of Mtali and alleged to be the true son of Mtali: the other produced by Manyasi, another brother of Mtali, reported by him to be the son of an older brother of Mtali. Mivanga and the Uganda chiefs were strongly inclined towards Manyasi's protégé, from the fact that he had always held cordial relations with Uganda: particularly since he induced Mtali to shelter the Christians at the time of their expulsion from Uganda by the Mohammedans. Kaish, on the other hand, had the reputation of being a turbulent character, strongly opposed to Uganda and—so the Uganda chiefs said—European influence in Ankole affairs. Manyasi was reported to have been driven out of Ankole, and to have taken refuge with the Pokino in Buddu, carrying with him a large herd of cattle.

"On the 17th October, a Muhima named Amani appeared at Kampala with envoys from Kaish and Gomira. The envoys begged for the support of H.M. Government and the King of Uganda (Kabaka of Buganda) for the son of Mtali. Whilst the matter was under discussion Manyasi himself appeared. When questioned, he denied the existence of the reputed son of Mtali. I asked Amani and the envoys if they were prepared to remain in Kampala whilst messengers were sent from the Government and the King. Amani and the envoys at once agreed. As representing the Government Mohamed Daud was sent. The King sent a Mkungu named Gidson and a chief of lower grade to assist him.

"The messengers have now returned, and individually and collectively report as follows:—

'At Lunga we met Kaish and Gomira together. The other chiefs had principally gone to fight Marinia, a pretender to the throne without any acknowledged claims,

---

[28] For the relationship between the claimants see the genealogical table, page viii.

who fled into German territory. We were directed to wait five days, Kaish being sick. We then met Kaish and Gomira again, who desired us to wait for the return of the war party, as they would then be able to represent the whole of the present Ankole territory. We waited nine days for this party to return. At the conference then held, there were present: Kaish and Gomira; Visa, Katikiro of Mtali; Gumaya, a second Katikiro; Gurakimitti, uncle of Mtali; Liamgwizi and Kazungu, brothers of Mtali, and others. The conference was unanimous in declaring that Mtali had given birth to a son by a woman who had died soon after childbirth. This woman, becoming pregnant, had been sent by Mtali to Gomira's wife to be delivered. There were witnesses to the negotiations between Mtali and the parents of the woman on the occasion of her becoming Mtali's wife. The chiefs in conference desired Mohamed Daud and Gidson, who had both seen Mtali, to identify Mtali's son by his likeness to Mtali out of a number of youths to be gathered together for the purpose. We waited two days. On the third day two bodies of people gathered near to us, and the chiefs appeared and asked us to carry out the wish of the conference. We had no difficulty in doing so: the son—for we now have no doubt he is such—being particularly recognisable from the projecting teeth and thick limbs peculiar to Mtali, besides of course a general likeness in features and expression. Kaish said he was sorry that Manyasi was absent as he was sure he would have waived his claims under these circumstances. The Ankole chiefs accuse Manyasi of having bolted with Mtali's cattle on the day of Mtali's death, and they will only agree to his residing again in Ankole on condition that he gives up the cattle to Mtali's heirs. Another conference was held and the chiefs have sent Dwakisaya and Kales, two of Mtali's known official messengers, with a large tusk of ivory weighing about 2½ frasilas to H.M. Government; and a small tusk and five head of cattle to Mwanga, besides minor presents to chiefs, as an earnest of their sincerity in begging support and protection in placing Mtali's son on the throne and in governing Ankole. Kaish and Gomira to be appointed guardians or regents. Kaish during these negotiations has been most cordial, and together with Gomira, has expressed the most earnest solicitude for the friendly assistance of the Government.'

"Manyasi is still in Mengo, but the King and Uganda chiefs now consider that his part is played out[29] and they support the claims of Mtali's son; being quite convinced from the evidence acquired by the messengers of the legitimate claims of Kaish's and Gomira's protégé."

Despite the fact that the envoys were entirely satisfied that Kahaya was Ntare's son, it is much more commonly believed in Ankole today that he was in fact the son of Igumira. Kahaya was, however, in general accepted as rightful Omugabe, Rwakatogoro's claim having little support.[30] Kahitsi who, with Igumira, ruled in Kahaya's name still hoped, however, to supplant his cousin.

In 1896 the Protectorate, which had previously comprised Buganda only, was extended so as to include Ankole as well as other territories to the west and east of Buganda. A despatch from the Foreign Office to the Commissioner dated 17 July, 1896, states as follows:

"The Marquis of Salisbury has given his careful consideration to the questions which have been raised on the subject of the difficulties as regards jurisdiction arising from the fact that Unyoro, Toro and Ankoli, though within the British sphere, were not included in the Protectorate.

"In order to regularise the situation, and to give Her Majesty's Commissioner the

---

9 Manyatsi was later killed while fighting for the Kabaka, Mwanga, after his dethronement.

0 Rwakatogoro's son, however, succeeded his cousin Kahaya in 1945 as the Omugabe Gasyonga II.

powers which are requisite for administration, it has been decided to add those territories to the Protectorate.

"The inclosed Notice was published in the 'London Gazette' of the 3rd instant By this measure the territories in question are brought within the jurisdiction conferred by the African Orders in Council.

"Extract from the 'London Gazette' of July 3rd, 1896:

Notice

The territory of Unyoro, together with that part of the British sphere of influence lying to the west of Uganda and Unyoro which has not hitherto been included in the Uganda Protectorate, is placed within the limits of that Protectorate, which includes, also, Usoga and the other territories to the east under the administration of Her Majesty's Commissioner and Consul-General for the Protectorate."

In 1897 the Kabaka Mwanga fled, first to Buddu and then to German territory, leaving behind a large body of supporters under his Mujasi Gabrielli. For the next couple of years these armed bands operating from Kabula, which was still part of Nkore or Ankole as it shall be referred to from now on, continued to be a source of trouble to the Protectorate Government and raided Buddu and the neighbouring country. Though the Government had an active supporter in a Mohammedan chief in Bukanga called Kahusi, the leading chiefs of Ankole either sympathised with the rebels or were powerless to resist them. In such circumstances it was essential for the Protectorate Government to have effective control over Ankole. Messengers from Kahitsi and Kahaya had expressed their wish for the support of the protecting power and, in December 1898, R. J. D. Macallister arrived to set up a civil station at Mbarara. A military force of one company was also stationed in the new district.

Macallister had various difficulties with which to contend. Kahitsi, who was forced to hand over Ntare's property to Kahaya, threatened rebellion and, like most of the Bahinda chiefs, was jealous of the power of the young Muhororo Enganzi, Mbaguta. There were still armed bands in Kabula against whom Macallister, with the small force at his disposal, was powerless. The situation was so difficult that at one time the evacuation of Ankole was even considered. Since the enforcement of law and order in Kabula was, inevitably, the responsibility of the authorities in Buganda, the country was, in September 1899, put under the control of a Muganda chief with the intention that it should in time be included in Buganda, and by the terms of the Agreement of 1900 Kabula became one of the Kabaka's counties. Worse, however, was to follow. The Buganda Regents managed to convince the Commissioner that Ankole, as well as other neighbouring territory, had, in previous years, been tributary to Buganda, and Macallister was informed that an annual tribute of fifty-five head of cattle, ten goats and eight tusks of ivory should be paid to Buganda. Macallister replied that no tribute had ever been paid by Ankole; that the imposition of tribute, following the annexation of Kabula, would have a disturbing effect; and that, if a tax were necessary, then a hut tax should be imposed by the Administration.

Macallister and his successor, R. R. Racey, who took over as Collector in 1900, were men of energy and determination. The country was extensively toured and rebellious chiefs were punished. The enthusiasm of these two administrators often alarmed the authorities in Entebbe who would write despatches (which it would appear were, as often as not, disregarded) warning the collectors that they must not drive "these volatile and excitable natives" too far, lest they should take themselves and their herds off into German territory, and that, if they could not administer without force, they must withdraw altogether. A typical rebuke, administered to Macallister in the form of a semi-official letter of June 1899, from Ternan, the Commissioner, reads as follows:

"I am sorry to see that you have had a military expedition in Ankole. Please bear in mind the necessity at present of keeping *quiet*. In no case can I send you further troops. If we can't hold Ankole without a row we must come out of it. F.O. (Foreign Office) *won't have* any more rows at present, and there will be trouble if their wishes are not complied with."

The discipline of the new régime, with which Mbaguta whole-heartedly co-operated, was not to the liking of many of the formerly all-powerful Bahinda chiefs, the leader of whom Igumira, now no longer virtual ruler of the country, the control of which was in the hands of the Collector and Mbaguta, was ill prepared to content himself merely with his chieftainship of Shema and part of Kashari. Racey found it impossible to control him and when Igumira attempted to seize a petty chieftainship belonging to his neighbour the Omukama of Igara, Racey in September 1900 arrested him and had him exiled from Ankole, his chieftainship and 150 head of confiscated cattle being handed over to Mbaguta. Trouble was expected when Igumira was removed but the only incident was the flight of Kijoma, the chief of Kikyenkye in North Kashari. Kijoma, a Muhinda, was a strong supporter of Igumira and when he heard of the latter's exile he determined to leave Ankole. An attempt was made by Racey to intercept and arrest him, but Kijoma speared the leader of the Collector's party and made good his escape together with his cattle across the German frontier.

The year prior to the Agreement of 1901 saw the steady expansion of the area effectively controlled by the Omugabe. Macallister and Racey accepted, perhaps too readily, the claims which Mbaguta and the other leading Ankole chiefs put forward on the Omugabe's behalf, and then sought to put them into effect. In this they were not altogether successful.

Despite Macallister's protests that Kitagwenda should pay tribute, it was incorporated as a saza in Toro, and neither Makobore, the head of the Beenekirenzi in Rujumbura, nor Rugarama, the head of the Beenekihondwa in Kajara, could be persuaded to accept the Omugabe as his overlord. Trouble in Bunyaruguru was settled by deposing Kuri-ofire and replacing him by Kaihura who had previously held only the chieftainship of Kazinga, and Kuri-ofire's land east of the Cambura was given to Buhweju.

In January 1901, an attempt was made to bring Musinga, the Omukama of Igara, into Mbarara to acknowledge Kahaya as his ruler. Musinga agreed to make the journey but custom decreed that Abakama should never meet one another. Furthermore, Musinga feared that he would suffer the same fate as his enemy Igumira. On reaching the Kandekye, which was the boundary of his kingdom, Musinga produced a hidden knife and disembowelled himself. On hearing of the Omukama's death, his sister, Kitunga, went to the royal kraal and ordered all the women to hang themselves. Then she hanged Musinga's two sons Mukotani and Kibwana, boys of about ten and seven years old, and finally she hanged herself. Fortunately, help came in time and the two boys were rescued alive. Mukotani was then installed as saza chief of Igara under the regency of his uncle Bakora.

By April, Racey was able to report that Ankole proper consisted of nine sazas, Isingiro, Nyabushozi, Mitoma, Nshara, Buzimba, Shema, Rwampara, Igara and Bunyaruguru. Four other areas, he added, had not yet been brought under the control of the Native Government, Rujumbura, Kajara, Buhweju and Bukanga. Concerning these, he made the following observations: "Rujumbura requires special attention. Kajara and Buhweju may come to terms in time and recognise Kahaya as Principal Chief. Bukanga is independent of Bahima local or native government by sanction of H.M. Commissioner."

In 1900 a clash had occurred between Kahusi, the Mohammedan chief of South Bukanga for whom the Administration had the highest regard, and Kanyabuzana the pagan chief of North Bukanga, during which Kahusi lost his life. Kanyabuzana whom the Banyankore regard as a national hero fled across the German frontier.[31] The whole of Bukanga was then put under a Muganda chief, Abdul Effendi, and was for the next seven years independent of Ankole. With its large population of immigrant Baganda, Bukanga was, during this period, nearly lost for good to Ankole and absorbed, like Kabula, in Buganda.

The mountainous kingdom of Buhweju was the next problem with

---

[31] Kanyabuzana had met Stanley in 1889 as Kiboga's envoy. He returned to Ankole after the 1914–18 war and ended his days as keeper of Ntare's tomb at Kaigoshora.

which Racey had to deal. Frightened and suspicious of the Europeans, Ndagara, now about eighty years old, refused to come to Mbarara or to allow a European to enter his kingdom, though he was quite prepared to send presents and messages of friendship. Racey was in a difficult position. On the one hand, he had been warned by the Commissioner that there must be no more aggression; nor did he wish to risk a second suicide by forcing Ndagara to come to Mbarara against his will. On the other hand, Lieutenant G. C. R. Mundy, the officer in charge of the military forces in the district, who was convinced that failure to enter Buhweju was discrediting the Administration in the eyes of the Banyankore, was constantly urging Racey to undertake a military expedition, whilst Mbaguta and the leading Banyankore chiefs were eager to see the kingdom subjected to the Omugabe's rule and may well for this purpose have made the most of difficulties which arose between Ndagara and the Collector. In April 1901, Racey, with an armed force which Mbaguta accompanied, entered Buhweju but, when Ndagara burnt his kraal and retired into the interior, the force withdrew. Ndagara then sent a relative, Igana, to make blood-brotherhood with Racey, but, when Igana returned after the ceremony, Ndagara, according to Mbaguta, disowned him.

In June, Mundy led a reconnaissance party into Buhweju and, so it was said, was given poisoned beer by Ndagara. Further provoked, Racey in July again entered Buhweju with the intention of bringing Ndagara to Mbarara. The expedition and its unhappy climax is tersely described by Racey in his monthly report for July:

"On the 1st instant a message from Wandagara Chief of Buhezu was delivered to me stating that if I again entered his country he would spear me. I sent him due warning accordingly and entered his country on the morning of the 12th accompanied by Inst. Wood and 60 constables. On arriving at his village of Kasungwi, Wandagara did not give himself up but went into an adjoining shamba with some of his followers where during an attempt to dislodge him he was shot with his son Chiga and a number of supporters who offered resistance as already reported. The cattle were temporarily removed as well as a number of women who might otherwise have committed suicide. Chiefs later came to arrange a settlement and were informed that they must acknowledge Kahia (Kahaya) as their principal chief as well as pay a fine of 300 spears. Luwarema (Ndibarema) the only surviving son of Wandagara was unanimously elected chief on 25th inst. by all the remaining chiefs of Buhezu who had come in bringing with them the fine of 300 spears. Luwarema after acknowledging Kahia and having handed over the spears, was made chief. The cattle and women temporarily removed were returned. I am of the opinion that there will be no further serious trouble in Buhezu."

It was inevitable that Racey should find himself in trouble for the Buhweju expedition. Wilson, now Sub-Commissioner of the Western Province, made a full inquiry into the incident. As a result of the inquiry he was satisfied that there had originally been no intention to fight, the purpose of the expedition being to surprise Ndagara as the result of a night march and to capture him and bring him to Mbarara. Owing to a miscalculation, the party did not reach Ndagara till after daybreak and the Omukama's forces were waiting for them and, not prepared to listen to Racey's attempt to parley, attacked the Collector's force of police. Wilson was certain that had Ndagara himself not fallen early in the conflict, thereby causing panic among his supporters, Racey's force would very probably have been overwhelmed by Ndagara's main army said to have been concealed in the rear of the action. If, however, the Sub-Commissioner thought Racey justified in his conduct of the expedition he did not think him so in undertaking it. "It was altogether ill advised of Mr. Racey," he says in an official report, "to go without orders into Wandagara's country. Of course fighting is not the work of a Collector and resorting to it implies failure in civil work. I can only say that in this case Mr. Racey has again shown a total misconception as to his position—in fact he seems to have placed no limit whatever upon the independence of action which he believed the Special Commission granted him."

The Omugabe had earlier in the year asked the Protectorate Government for a formal Agreement on the lines of that signed in Toro the previous year.   At the time it was thought that Ankole was not yet sufficiently settled to justify this, but now that Buhweju had been subjugated to the Omugabe and all the present district except the south-west recognised the British Administration, it was felt that the time was ripe. On 7 August, 1901, the Ankole Agreement between Frederick Jackson on behalf of the Government of the United Kingdom on the one hand and the Omugabe and his chiefs on the other was, accordingly, signed at Mbarara. This Agreement which was modelled on that of Toro bears little resemblance to the Buganda Agreement and is a short and simple document. It does little more than recognise the Omugabe as "Kabaka or supreme chief" over all of what is now Ankole District, except Bukanga and Kajara; define the saza boundaries, confirming the saza chiefs in their positions and giving them the right to nominate their successors; vest all uncultivated land at that time unallocated and all forests and minerals in His Majesty's Government; provide for the imposition of a hut tax and gun tax whilst preventing the levying of any exactions by chiefs, ten per cent of these taxes being payable to the chief who collected them; state that justice between Africans of the district is to be administered by the saza chiefs; and allocate freehold estates to the Omugabe and saza chiefs.[32]

---

[32] For the text of the Agreement see the Appendix.

Chapter IX
1901 TO 1914

THE Agreement of 1901 left Mbaguta in a stronger position than ever for by it he was confirmed in the saza chieftainships of Shema and Kashari, where Igumira had ruled before his exile, together with that of Ngarama which both he and his grandfather had ruled in the previous century, as well as holding the post of Enganzi.[33] Mbaguta despite later differences with the Omugabe, who as he grew to manhood resented his rather overbearing Enganzi, was the dominant personality in Ankole for three and a half decades. Intelligent, imperious and courageous, he was a firm believer in progress and a sincere Christian. Ankole owes to Mbaguta a deep debt of gratitude for the part he played in guiding the country smoothly through the transitionary period from the traditional tribal society to that of the modern world, a part comparable to that played by Apolo Kagwa in Buganda.

The majority of the saza chiefs who signed the Agreement, or at any rate their nominated successors, unlike Mbaguta, were unable to adapt themselves to the new régime and did not survive the first few years which followed the Agreement. In 1902 both Matsiko, the saza chief of Nyabushozi, and Mazinyo (Rukuratwa) of Isingiro were dismissed by H. St. G. Galt, who had taken over from Racey as Collector a month after the Agreement was signed, on account of inefficiency. In the same year Nduru ceased to be saza chief of Buzimba. Nduru found it impossible to adapt himself to the role of an administrative chief in a county which he had previously ruled as Omukama and Galt in 1901 appointed as his "Katikiro" the able young Muhinda Henry Ryamugwizi. Nduru resented the intrusion of this stranger and appointed his own "Katikiro", Mucukura his brother, Ryamugwizi being left to enforce the unpopular government measures such as collection of hut tax and labour on the roads. After

---

[33] The family history of Mbaguta as recounted by himself is given by F. Lukyn Williams in "Nuwa Mbaguta, Nganzi of Ankole", *Uganda Journal*, Vol. 10, 1946. Rwamahe, Mbaguta's grandfather, was one of the Beeneishemurari to be driven out of Kajara into Shema. Rwamahe's sister married the Omugabe Rwebishengye and Rwamahe later went to his brother-in-law's court and was given the chieftainships of Bukanga and Ngarama. Both Rwamahe and Mbaguta's father, Rwabubi, were killed fighting for Ntare against the Baganda who were supporting Mukwenda. After Ntare's victory over his brother, Mbaguta served at his court, becoming Enganzi at the end of the Omugabe's reign.

Mbaguta held his chieftainships until 1924, when he was induced to surrender them and to devote himself to the work of Enganzi alone. He finally retired in 1937 and died in 1944.

a few months. Nduru found his position intolerable and resigned, departing with his cattle across the Toro border; Ryamugwizi was thereupon appointed saza chief in his place. It was also in 1901 that Kaihura of Bunyaruguru died leaving as heir his son Kasigano. Kasigano, however, soon got into trouble: he became involved with the Belgians in disputes about the frontier and when one of the Omugabe's askaris was skilled he fled into Belgian territory and in 1906 was dismissed, the county being for a time placed directly under Mbaguta's control. Two more of the signatories to the Agreement also died in these early years of the new administration, Rutasharara of Nshara[34] and Bucunku of Mitoma, whilst in 1908 Mukotani of Igara also came to grief. A Muganda was murdered in his compound and Mukotani was held responsible, was imprisoned for a short while and was dismissed from his saza.

The removal by dismissal or death of so many of the senior chiefs at this time greatly strengthened Mbaguta's hand. Although he was one again to encounter for a short while the opposition of Igumira, the champion of the old regime, who was allowed to return to Ankole in 1903, his position, whilst he retained the confidence of the Collector, was secure. To Mbaguta fell the task of persuading the native government of the Omugabe and his chiefs to accept reforms initiated by the protecting power and often unpalatable to the traditional leaders. Of these reforms perhaps the most important was the decision, to which the Omugabe and his chiefs were persuaded to agree in 1904, that all cattle in Ankole at that date should henceforth be held to belong to those in whose hands they were at the time. This decision, which deprived the wealthy Bahima chiefs of the ultimate possession of considerable herds, was, needless to say, highly unpopular with them.

The Church Missionary Society had arrived in the district in 1901, followed by the White Fathers Mission in 1902, and both the Omugabe and Mbaguta had very soon accepted baptism followed by most of the leading chiefs. Under the able lead of Mbaguta the authority of the British Administration and of the Omugabe was accepted throughout the district apart from the unsettled and still unadministered area of the south-west and, with the Missions established in their work of evangelisation and education, a period of steady progress seemed to lie ahead. It therefore came as a great shock to the Administration when, in 1905, a senior administrative officer was murdered in the district, especially since the murder was believed to have had political implications. [35]

---

[34]   Rutashara nominated as his successor in Nshara his nephew Kazine but the latter
        was found unstable and was reduced to the rank of a gombolola chief in 1907.
[35]   For a detailed account of this case see H.F. Morris, "The Murder of H.St. G. Galt",
        Uganda Journal, Vol. 24, 1960.

In May 1905 Galt, who was then acting as Sub-Commissioner of the Western Province,[36] was spending a night in a rest-house near Ibanda when a man entered the compound, threw a spear at him as he sat on the verandah and killed him.

A detailed inquiry, lasting nearly a month, was held at Ibanda under the direction of Wilson, then Deputy Commissioner, the rulers and leading chiefs of both Ankole and Toro being present throughout. From the start, Wilson was certain that the murder was not an isolated incident of revenge but had a political motive behind it and he was baffled by the sullen opposition with which his inquiry was met. The Toro and Ankole chiefs, apart from trying to throw the blame upon the other's district, had little help to offer. Various possible motives, the exile of Igumira and the loss of his chieftainships, the death of Ndagara of Buhweju, the flight of Kijoma, the suicide of Musinga and the replacement of Nduru as saza chief of Buzimba were pursued but led nowhere. At one time, Mucukura, Nduru's brother, was under suspicion but the case against him turned out to be groundless. Then suddenly, a week after the inquiry had started, a man informed Wilson that the murderer was a peasant called Rutaraka. Then it was rumoured that Rutaraka had committed suicide and the authorities were led to his grave. It appeared on examination of the body that, in fact, his death had not been self-inflicted but that he had been murdered. Wilson was still certain that persons more important than peasants had been responsible for Galt's murder and his suspicions now turned on Rwakakaiga,[37] the saza chief of Mitoma, and Nyakayaga, a sub-chief of the Ibanda area. Neither of these chiefs had assisted as they should have done in the inquiry and, on Wilson's orders, they were arrested and investigations were made into their conduct as a result of which they were found to have acted with "the most culpable negligence and indifference" and to have suppressed "knowledge which would have been of the greatest use towards securing the murderer of Rutaraka". They were, accordingly, placed under close arrest.

By the end of June there was still no evidence to show who had been behind the murder and Wilson, in despair, gave orders for the members of the inquiry to move to Hoima. All was ready for Wilson's departure, when a Muhima, Bitabi, came to him with the following story. Some time previously, Bitabi said, he had taken milk to Rwakakaiga and, at a drinking party, had heard him offer a reward for the death of a European.

---

36 Galt was succeeded as Collector of Ankole in 1903 by C. E. Dashwood, who in the following year handed over to F. A. Knowles.
37 When Bucunku of Mitoma had died of smallpox earlier in the year, he had nominated his cousin and fellow Muhinda, Gabrielli Rwakakaiga, as his successor.

Rwakakaiga had added, so Bitabi said, that this was to be in revenge for the death of Manyatsi and also for the death of his cousin Bucunku who had been given smallpox by the magic of the Europeans. This statement was later supported, in broad outline, by several other witnesses. Furthermore, one, Ndolere, admitted that he, with the help of two others, had killed Rutaraka on Nyakayaga's orders.

Rwakakaiga and Nyakayaga were, accordingly, tried by the High Court for abetting the murder of Galt committed by Rutaraka.[38] The prosecution case rested mainly on the evidence of five witnesses, all of whom testified as to conversations which they had taken part in or had overheard. The evidence they gave was vivid and detailed but was also bewildering for, although, in general, their evidence agreed that a reward had been offered by the accused for the death of a European as a revenge for Bucunku's death, yet the details as to where and when these conversations took place and as to who were present at them, differed very considerably. The judge, however, was satisfied that the evidence of a conspiracy between the two accused to commit murder was convincing and convicted them and sentenced them to death. Appeal was then made to the Court of Appeal of East Africa. Two of the appeal judges in a majority verdict tore to shreds the judgment of the trial court and reversed its decision. In their opinion the witnesses had only come into court after much pressure had been brought to bear on them, whilst some of them had motives for laying the blame on the accused. Furthermore, if their story were true, they were accomplices and their evidence was, therefore, entitled to no weight unless corroborated independently. The third appeal judge, however, submitted a minority judgment, not because he disagreed with his colleagues' decision, but with many of their arguments. He was not at all sure that the witnesses had been lying for they might have remembered parts only of the conversations they had heard, whilst their statements had often come through two interpreters. He did not, however, think that the case against the accused had been conclusively proved and he therefore agreed that the judgment must be reversed. Wilson, who at the time was Acting Commissioner, was amazed when he heard of the acquittal and, convinced that it was necessary for the peace and good order of the country that the two chiefs should be exiled, he had them deported in January 1906 to Kismayu, then in the East African Protectorate.[39] Igumira, whom Wilson also suspected of being implicated in the crime, was banished from

---

[38] Although it was assumed throughout the trial and afterwards that the actual murder was committed by Rutaraka, this is by no means certain.
[39] Now in Somaliland. Rwakakaiga died there in 1916. In 1925 Nyakayaga was allowed to return to Uganda provided he lived at Jinja; in 1928 he was allowed back to Ankole.

Nuwa Mbaguta
(*from a painting by Margaret Trowell*)

The drums of Igara. Rwamyaniko, the hereditary keeper of the drums (left) is seen with E. Rukunyu, the head of the Beenemafundo. Mazima, consort to Kihoza, is the drum in front of Rwamyaniko; to the right is the main drum, Kihoza. The undecorated drums are attendants to Kihoza and Mazima.

Ankole for the second time and died an impoverished exile in Buganda in 1925.

No further evidence ever came to light and the background to the murder, and in particular the real reason why it was committed, remains a mystery. A few months after the murder, the Agreement was suspended. This apparently was done not merely as a punishment but because it was thought that under the terms of the Agreement it was not possible for the murderers of Rutaraka to be tried by the High Court.[40] The Secretary of State for the Colonies, however, in giving his approval to the suspension pointed out that this was not so since the High Court had full jurisdiction over all persons and matters; he added that since it was not clear that there had been any infringement of the Agreement such as would justify its annulment under Section 3, the suspension must "be regarded as an act of force justified by the necessity of marking the gravity of the crime". The Omugabe and the saza chiefs of Ankole were fined one thousand one hundred head of cattle and the people of the Ankole sazas of Buhweju, Buzimba and Mitoma and of the Toro saza of Kitagwenda had to pay double poll tax for the year. The greatest hardship which the people of Mitoma suffered as a consequence of the murder, however, was, undoubtedly, the appointment, in Rwakakaiga's place, of the Muganda Abdul Aziz Bulwada, who had been Wilson's interpreter during the inquiry at Ibanda, as saza chief. His tyrannical rule lasted till 1908 when his barbaric treatment of his people led to his dismissal.

In those parts of Ankole which lay within easy reach of Mbarara and were capable of close administration, there was steady progress during the succeeding years. In the wilder regions of south-west Shema and south-west Igara which lay close to the frontier of Belgian territory, remote from the civil station at Mbarara, the authority of the Omugabe and of the Collector was slight and for several years incidents of lawlessness occurred necessitating the sending into the area of armed patrols of police. Still more remote were the areas of Kajara and Rujumbura. Although within the British sphere of influence, no clear boundary with German and Belgian territory had yet been demarcated and, largely through fear of international incidents, the Collector at Mbarara had been instructed by the Commissioner that this area should be left alone and, although the Collectors had some dealings with the chiefs of these parts, there was for the time being no

---

40 Section 6 of the Agreement states that: "Justice as between native and native shall be administered direct by the recognised chiefs. . . . " In the opinion of the Protectorate Government, this precluded trial in a Protectorate court where both the accused and the victim were Africans. Such an argument did not of course apply to the main case of Galt's murder.

attempt to impose the poll tax on the area or in any other way to administer it.

Although the revenue of the district rose steadily year by year,[41] the efforts of the Administration to increase its wealth by the introduction of cash crops was, during these years, almost completely unsuccessful. First wheat was introduced and then cotton. Although the prospects for cotton at first looked bright, the early promise was not fulfilled and the annual amount of this crop which had risen to 27,000 lb. in 1911-2, had fallen virtually to nothing by 1914. By this time a few chiefs and others had also started the cultivation of coffee, but the real trouble was that without proper roads, and there were virtually none in the district fit to carry wheeled transport, it was impossible to develop trade and to provide any incentive to the peasant to grow crops for sale. As late as 1914, the wealth of the country lay almost entirely in its livestock which, together with skins and ghee, formed practically the sole exports of the district. The days of the greatness of Ankole's grazing lands and of her herds were, however, already numbered. By 1913, trypanosomiasis had spread from German territory into what is now the southern part of Isingiro and the immigration of a large number of cattle owners with their cattle from the fly-ridden area south of the Kagera on the outbreak of war hastened the advance of the disease. The Provincial Commissioner's annual report for the year 1914-5 tells of the first steps to be taken by bush clearance in the long and none too successful battle against the fly which has continued ever since.

The period between Galt's murder and the outbreak of war was to see a number of important administrative reforms. In 1907 a subsidiary Agreement was entered into whereby the Omugabe and the saza chiefs agreed that all indefinite contributions and services due from a peasant to his chief should be replaced by a yearly payment of Rupees 2 or one month's labour instead.[42] In 1910 the Poll Tax Ordinance was applied to Ankole under which every male adult had to pay a tax of Rupees 5 in place of the old hut tax. In the following year the native courts were constituted under the Native Courts Ordinance. The three levels of courts which exist today were thereby recognised with jurisdiction over Africans of the Protectorate and immigrants from across the German border, the "Court of the Lukiko" having the power to hear all cases except those punishable with death or transportation for life. In 1912 the Agreement of 1901, which had been suspended after Galt's death, was restored subject to the fact that "such restoration shall not invalidate the Poll Tax introduced

---

[41] In the year March 1905–March 1906 the revenue of the district was Rupees 51,236; in 1913–4 it was Rupees 268,430.
[42] For the text of the Agreement see the Appendix.

by Proclamation of the 13th May 1910 nor the system of courts and the authority vested in them by the Proclamation of the 31st March 1911 or any act or order of Government whatsoever done or issued during the suspension of the said Agreement".

In 1907 Abdul Effendi agreed to become one of the Omugabe's chiefs and Bukanga once more became a part of Ankole. It was not, however, until some years later that the western boundary of Ankole was settled. That part of the old kingdom of Mpororo which comprised the present sazas of Kajara and Rujumbura was considered both by the Native Government and by the early Collectors to be part of the Omugabe's kingdom, although it was not included within the boundaries laid down by the Agreement and remained unadministered for reasons which have already been given. Contact had however been made by the Collectors with Makobore, the Mwenekirenzi chief of Rujumbura, but he steadfastly refused to acknowledge the Omugabe as his ruler, maintaining, with justice it would seem, that his ancestors had never been subordinate to Nkore. When the dispute as to the boundary in the extreme south-west of the Protectorate was finally settled, to Uganda's considerable advantage, and the new district of Kigezi was set up in 1912 for the administration of the area, Makobore elected to have his country included in this district rather than in Ankole.

Rugarama, the Mwenekihondwa chief of Kajara, was in a difficult position. The Anglo-German Boundary Commission, 1902-4, which, in accordance with the Anglo-German Agreement of 1890, demarcated the boundary along the parallel of latitude 1° south, put a large part of his country in German territory. Although friendly towards the British Administration, Rugarama found it hard to make up his mind in which part of his country he would live. He was in any case an ineffectual chief, unable to control his subordinates, and when the administration of Kajara was undertaken it was found impossible to leave him in sole control. In 1909, Rwenkaranga, a relation of Mbaguta, was appointed as saza chief over Rugarama. Very soon there was friction between the new chief and Rugarama. One of Rugarama's chiefs was killed at Rwenkaranga's instigation and Rugarama fled for German territory pursued by Rwenkaranga with three hundred followers. At the frontier Rugarama and his band turned upon their pursuers and killed Rwenkaranga and practically exterminated his force. A Muganda was then made saza chief and Rugarama faded out as an effective force in Kajara. Finally, in 1914, the boundary was altered in Ankole's favour, the southern portion of the Beenekihondwa territory, together with the Bagina lands of Butaya, being incorporated in Kajara saza. With this frontier adjustment, Ankole reached its furthest limits and the era of expansion which had lasted two centuries was over.

APPENDIX

TEXTS OF THE TREATIES

A. THE TREATY OF 1891

I, Bireri, the son of Ntali, King of Ankole, and successor to his title, having been sent by my father Ntali to make blood-brotherhood and conclude a treaty with Captain F. D. Lugard, 9th Regiment, D.S.O., acting solely on behalf of the Imperial British East Africa Company, having been fully authorised by Ntali to act in every way as his representative, all my acts and undertakings being binding on him; whereof Zacharia Kagolo (signatory as witness to this Treaty) and Ali, Somali headman, the envoys to Ntali from Captain Lugard, and those present who have been sent with me from my father's capital are witnesses. I, therefore, Bireri, having this day made blood-brotherhood with Captain F. D. Lugard, do undertake, in the name of my father, that he and his successor shall be friends of the British. He himself does acknowledge that his territories are under British suzerainty, in recognition whereof I have this day accepted on his behalf the flag of the Company as a symbol of their authority. And I do hereby undertake to do all in my power to prevent the import of arms and ammunition in British Territory from the south, viz into Uganda, Unyoro and the countries to the north; and to seize such powder as I may find being carried through my country for the purpose of those countries, and to deal severely with those who bring it. And I agree not to allow any Europeans to settle in my country except the British; and to inform the Resident at Mengo, or the nearest British Representative, if any European, not in the Company's employment, shall enter or pass through my country. And towards the Company and its employees there shall be entire friendship from me and all my people, and they shall be welcome to pass through my country, or to build in it; and all facilities shall be given them for buying food, and for peaceful passage through my country and for trading and settling; and the enemies of the Company shall be my enemies. And these things I, Bireri, son of Ntali, undertake on behalf of Ntali, King of Ankole, and in token thereof I have attached my mark to this Treaty.

And I, Captain F. D. Lugard, 9th Regiment, on behalf of the Imperial British East Africa Company, do, in return for these promises and undertakings on the part of Ntali, King of Ankole, hereby promise to him and

46

his successors the friendship of the said Company so long as they abide by the terms of the Treaty.

Signed this 1st day of July, 1891, at Nabusossi in Ankole
(signed) F. D. LUGARD, Captain 9th Regiment.
          BIRERI, his X mark, son of Ntali of Ankole.

Witness:
(signed) W. GRANT, Imperial British East Africa Company.

Interpreters and witness:
(signed) ZAKARIA KAGOLO, Sub-Chief in Uganda.
          DUALLA.
          YAFETI, his X mark, Sub-Chief of Uganda and Unyoro.

B. THE TREATY OF 1894

Treaty made at Ntali's in Ankoli, this 29th day of August, in the year 1894, between Major Cunningham, Derby Regiment, for Colonel Colvile, C.B., for and on behalf of Her Majesty the Queen of Great Britain and Ireland, Empress of India etc., her heirs and successors, on the one part, and the Undersigned, Magota, Katikiro, of Ntali, King of Ankoli, for his (Ntali's) heirs and successors, on the other part.

I, the Undersigned, Magota, do, in the presence of the Headmen and people assembled at this place, hereby promise:—

1. That there shall be peace between the subjects of the Queen of England and Ntali's subjects.

2. That British subjects shall have free access to all parts of Ankoli, and shall have the right to build houses and possess property according to the laws in force in this country; that they shall have full liberty to carry on such trade or manufacture as may be approved by Her Majesty; and should any difference arise between the aforesaid British subjects and Ntali, the said King of Ankoli, as to the duties or customs to be paid to Ntali the said King or the Headmen of the towns in Ankoli country by such British subjects or as to any other matter, that the dispute shall be referred to a duly authorised Representative of Her Majesty, whose decision in the matter shall be binding and final; and that Ntali will not extend the rights thus guaranteed to British subjects to any other persons without the knowledge and consent of such Representative.

3. That Ntali, the said King, will at no time whatever cede any of

Ankoli territory to any other Power, or enter into any Agreement, Treaty, or Arrangement with any foreign Government except through and with the consent of the Government of Her Majesty the Queen of England etc.

Done at Ntali's, this 29th day of August 1894
(signed) G. CUNNINGHAM, Major.
           MAGOTA, his X mark.

Signed in the presence of
    SAID ABD-EL-RAHMAN, MULAZIM

I, the Undersigned, do swear that I have truly and honestly interpreted the terms of the foregoing Agreement to the Contracting Parties in the Mhuma language.

Witness to signatures:
(signed) SAID ABD-EL-RAHMAN, MULAZIM, his X mark.

C. THE AGREEMENT OF 1901[43]

Between Frederick J. Jackson Esquire, C.B., His Majesty's Acting Commissioner and Consul-General for the Uganda Protectorate and the adjoining territories, representing the Government of His Britannic Majesty the King of Great Britain and Ireland and Emperor of India on the one part; and the Kabaka and Chiefs of the District of Ankole on the other part.

1. That portion of the District of Ankole to which the present Agreement applies shall be divided into the following administrative divisions

(a) Mitoma
(b) Nyabushozi
(c) Nshara
(d) Ishingiro
(e) Ruampara
(f) Buzimba
(g) Ngarama, Shema and Kashari
(h) Igara
(i) Buhwezho and
(j) Bunyaraguru.

---

[43] The text of the Agreement here quoted is as in the original and differs somewhat from that published in the Laws of Uganda, 1951, particularly with regard to the saza boundaries. The reason for this is that the latter text incorporates subsequent amendments made to the Agreement. These amending Agreements were entered into in 1914, 1923, 1924 and 1934. That of 1923 dealt with the sazas in which the Omugabe could have his private estates and the others dealt with alterations to the saza boundaries. In 1941 a subsidiary Agreement was entered into stipulating that in future alterations in saza boundaries could be effected by agreement between the Governor and the Omugabe without the need for a formal amending Agreement.

They shall be approximately bounded as follows—

The administrative division of Mitoma shall be bounded on the north by the recognised Ankole-Toro and Ankole-Uganda boundaries; on the east by the recognised Ankole-Uganda boundary; on the south by a line drawn due west between Rutunga on the north and Butaka on the south, to the Nyanza River, thence in a west-south-westerly direction north of Nyabisheche and south of Wakahaya to the Kabobo river, thence north-east to the Charutanga river following the recognised boundary, i.e. the portions of the rivers Orwibu, Katho and Charutanga, lying west of Ibanda, as far north as Fort Grant site.

The administrative division of Nyabushozi shall be bounded as follows—

On the north by the southern boundary of the administrative division of Mitoma; on the east by the recognised Uganda-Ankole boundary to the present Government Road; on the south by a line drawn due west north of Nsongi, thence by a line drawn due south-west to Mbarara station; on the west by a line drawn north-east by north from Mbarara station to south of Echitoma village, thence due west to the river Kabari, thence north following the rivers Kabari, Rubindi and Chandahi to the river Kabobo.

The administrative division of Nshara shall be bounded as follows—
On the north by the southern boundary of Nyabushozi, on the east by the recognised Ankole-Uganda boundary; on the south by a line passing through the centre of Lakes Kachera and Mazinga in a south-westerly direction, including the islands of Shangi and Kabagarira (sometimes peninsulas) to the mouth of the Ruizi river, and thence westwards along that river to Mbarara station.

The administrative division of Ishingiro shall be bounded as follows—
On the north by the Orwizi River; on the south-east by Lake Mazinga; on the south and south-west by the present government road.

The administrative division of the Ruampara shall be bounded as follows—

On the north by the River Orwizi; on the north-east and east by the present government road leading from Mbarara Station to Charubikwa leaving the Charubikwa shambas on the east, thence in a straight line due south to the Anglo-German boundary; on the south by the recognised Anglo-German boundary; on the west by the recognised Kazara-Ruampara boundary.

The administrative division of Buzimba shall be bounded as follows—
On the north by the recognised Toro-Ankole boundary; on the

east by a line drawn from the site of Fort Grant in a south and south-easterly direction following the Rivers Charutanga, Katho (swamp), Bufunda, Kabari I, Kabobo, Rubindi, Chandahi, and Kabari II, to the village of Rubindi; on the south by a line drawn due east and west from the village of Rubindi to Nyaruchika, including these two places; on the west and south-west by the recognised Buhwezho-Buzimba boundary.

The administrative divisions of Ngarama, Shema and Kashari shall be bounded as follows—

The administrative sub-division of Ngarama shall be bounded on the north by Lake Mazinga, on the east by the recognised Ankole-Bukanga boundary, i.e., by a line drawn through the valley running due south from Lake Mazinga to the Anglo-German boundary east of and at the foot of the hills Luametelengo and Luenkungulu; on the south by the Anglo-German boundary; on the west by the eastern boundary of the administrative division of the Ruampara. The administrative sub-divisions of Shema and Kashari shall be bounded on the north by a line running due east and west along the southern boundary of the administrative division of Buzimba to Echitoma village leaving Echitoma village on the north; on the east by a line drawn from the south of Echitoma village in a south by westerly direction to the Orwizi River; on the west by the Shema-Igara and Shema-Buhwezho boundaries.

The administrative division of Igara shall be bounded as follows— On the north by a line drawn along the top of a chain of hills lying directly north of that forest known as the Bunyaraguru Forest in an easterly direction to the Buhwezho-Igara recognised boundary, thence south-east to the head waters of the Orwizi river; on the east by the Shema-Igara boundary; on the south by the recognised Igara-Kazara and Igara-Ruzumburu boundaries; on the west by the recognised Igara-Ruzumburu, Igara-Ndusi, and Igara-Kamsusa boundaries.

The administrative division of Buhwezho shall be bounded as follows— On the north by Dweru Channel and Lake Dweru; on the east by the recognised Buhwezho-Buzimba and Buhwezho-Shema boundaries; on the south by the recognised Buhwezho-Igara boundary; on the west by the River Chambura.

The administrative division of Bunyaraguru shall be bounded as follows—

On the north-west by the Dweru Channel; on the east by the Chambura River, the recognised Bunyaraguru-Igara and Kamsusa-

Igara boundaries; on the south by the Rwenchwera river; on the west by Lake Albert Edward.

. The above defined administrative divisions do not include the whole area f the district of Ankole, but those portions of the district which border more losely on the Congo Free State and German Territory will be subject to the ame regulations as these set forth in this Agreement, and will for the present e administered by the principal European official placed in civil charge of ae Ankole district, until such time as the chiefs therefore voluntarily place aemselves under the suzerainship of Kahia.

. By this Agreement the Chief Kahaya is recognised by His Majesty's iovernment as the Kabaka or supreme chief over all that part of the nkole district which is included within the limits of the above-mentioned dministrative sub-divisions. Buchunku is recognised as chief over the Iitoma sub-division; Masiko is recognised as chief over the Nyabushozi sub-ivision; Rutasharara is recognised as the chief over the Nshara sub-division; Iazinyo is recognised as the chief over the Ishingiro sub-division; Duhara is ecognised as the chief over the Ruampara sub-division; Nduru is recognised s chief over the Buzimba sub-division; Baguta Katikiro is recognised as the hief over the Ngarama, and Shema and Kashari sub-divisions; Mkotani is ecognised as chief over the Igara sub-division (to be temporarily administered y Regent Bakara until such time as Mkotani shall come of age); Rubaremma aall be recognised as chief over Buhwezho sub-division; and Kaihura shall e recognised as chief over Bunyaruguru sub-division.

So long as the aforesaid Kabaka and chiefs abide by the conditions of this greement they shall continue to be recognised by His Majesty's Government s the responsible chiefs of the Ankole district.

They shall be allowed to nominate their successors in the event of their emise, and the successors thus nominated shall be in like manner recognised y His Majesty's Government as the successor to the dignity of chieftainship, n the understanding that they equally abide by the terms of this Agreement.

But should the Kabaka or the other chiefs herein named fail at any time to oide by any portion of the terms of this Agreement, they may be deposed by is Majesty's principal representative in the Uganda Protectorate, and their tles and privileges will then pass to any such other chiefs as His Majesty's incipal representatives may select in their place.

Should the Kabaka of Ankole – Kahaya or his successors – be responsi-le for the infringement of any part of the terms of this Agreement, it shall e open to His Majesty's Government to annual the said Agreement, and to substitute for it any other methods of administering the Ankole district which may seem suitable.

4.   All the waste and uncultivated land which is waste and uncultivated at the date of this Agreement, all forests, mines, minerals, and salt deposits in the Ankole district shall be considered to be the property of His Majesty's Government, the revenue derived therefrom being included within the general revenue of the Uganda Protectorate; but the natives of the Ankole district shall have the same privileges with regard to the forests as have been laid down and formulated in the aforesaid regulations in force in the Uganda Protectorate as are applicable to the natives of each province or other administrative division of the Protectorate within such province or administrative division.

His Majesty's Government shall have the right of enforcing on the natives of the Ankole district, as elsewhere in the Uganda Protectorate, the protection of game; and in this particular it is hereby agreed that within the Ankole district the elephant shall be strictly protected, and that the killing or capture of elephants on the part of the natives of the Ankole district shall be regulated by the Sub-Commissioner of the Western Province.

5.   There shall be imposed henceforth on the natives of the Ankole district the same taxation as is in force by proclamation in the other provinces or districts of the Uganda Protectorate, to wit, the hut tax and the gun tax.

All revenue derived from customs duties, hut taxes, gun taxes, salt deposits, or any other sources whatever, shall be paid direct to the principal officer in civil charge of the Ankole district.

No chief in the Ankole district shall henceforth levy on other chiefs or on natives tribute or gifts of any kind, except such as may be directly sanctioned by His Majesty's principal representatives in the Uganda Protectorate and as are specified in the clauses of this agreement.

6.   Justice as between native and native shall be administered direct by the recognised chiefs of the ten sub-divisions.   In all cases where a sentence of over three months' imprisonment, or a fine exceeding £5 in value, or where property of over £5 in value is concerned, an appeal shall lie from the divisional native Courts to the Lukiko of the Kabaka of Ankole.

In cases where the imprisonment exceeds a term of one year, or property involved exceeds the value of £100, an appeal shall lie from the decision of the Kabaka or his Lukiko to the principal European officer in civil charge of the district of Ankole.

All fines, fees, or other sums legitimately collected in the divisional native Courts of the district of Ankole shall be dealt with as follows—

One-third of the total annual value of these sums shall be retained by the local chief administering justice and two-thirds shall be remitte o the Kabaka of Ankole. All cases between natives of the district of Ankole and natives of the other districts of the Uganda Protectorate, r between natives and foreigners, shall be tried by the British magistrates n the district of Ankole, and shall be removed altogether from native jurisdiction.

7. From out of the total annual revenue received in the shape of gun es and hut taxes from the ten administrative divisions above specified he Ankole district, 10 per cent of the total value shall be paid to the baka, and of the total value of taxes remitted by the chief of each sub-ision, 10 per cent shall be remitted to the recognised chief of such sub-ision. Thus the Kabaka of Ankole will receive 10 per cent of the total ue of taxes collected in the ten previously mentioned sub-divisions of Ankole district; the chief of the Mitoma sub-division will receive 10 per t of the total value of the taxes collected in the Mitoma sub-division; chief of the Nyabushozi sub-division will receive 10 per cent of the ul value of the taxes collected in the Nyabushozi sub-division, and so h.

In addition to the percentage of the taxes, the Kabaka of Ankole, Kabaka, shall be granted an estate from out of the waste lands of the ma and Kashari sub-division of an area of 16 square miles, provided, vever, that such estate may not include within its limits any large area forest or salt or mineral deposit.

The Katikiro, or principal minister of the Kabaka of Ankole, shall, his official position as Katikiro, enjoy the usufruct of an estate to be tted out of the waste lands of the Shema and Kashari sub-division, in area of 10 square miles, not, however, to include any large forest iny salt or mineral deposit within its limits. The recognised chiefs of other nine sub-divisions of the Ankole district shall enjoy in their official acity the usufruct of an estate of 10 square miles from out of the waste is in their respective sub-divisions.

The private estates to be guaranteed to Kahaya, the present Kabaka Ankole, shall not exceed 50 square miles in area of which amount 25 are miles must be held in the sub-division of Sema and Kasari.

The private estate of the Katikiro shall not exceed 12 square miles, those of each existing chief of a sub-division as named in this Agreement, quare miles each.

In all respects the Ankole district will be subjected to the same laws regulations as are generally in force throughout the Uganda Protectorate.

Signed by the within-named Frederick J. Jackson, Esq., at Entebbe, on the 25th day of October, 1901.

F. J. JACKSON.

Witness:

A. G. BOYLE.

And by the Kabaka and Chiefs of Ankole at Mbarara on the 7th day of August, 1901.

> KAHAYA.
> BAGUTA.
> KAIHURA, his X mark.
> DUHARA, his X mark.
> NDURU, his X mark.
> BUCHUNKU, his X mark.
> RUTASHARARA, his X mark.
> MASIKO, his X mark.
> MAZINYO, his X mark.
> RUBAREMMA, his X mark.
> MKOTANI, his X mark.
> And his Regent,
> > BAKORA, his X mark.

Witnesses to signatures:

GEORGE WILSON,
Sub-Commissioner for the Western Province.

R. R. RACEY,
Collector, Ankole.

G. C. R. MUNDY, Lieutenant,
Commanding Ankole Military District.

J. J. WILLIS,
Church Missionary Society.

Interpreters:

SEMIONI, K.
ISAKA.

Note

With reference to gun and hut taxes to be imposed henceforth in the district of Ankole, the following exemptions and privileges will be granted annually to the personages named in this note: provided such personages adhere strictly to the terms of the Agreement entered into by the Kabaka and Chiefs of Ankole with the British Government—

The Kabaka of Ankole will be granted exemption from hut tax for 50 huts or houses.

The Katikiro of Ankole will be granted exemption for 35 huts or houses.

The recognised chiefs of each of the other nine administrative sub-divisions of the district of Ankole (as mentioned in the Agreement) will be granted severally exemption from hut tax for 25 huts or houses.

The Mujasi, or head of the Kabaka's police, shall be granted exemption for 10 huts or houses.

The following exemptions from payment of the gun taxes will be granted under the like conditions as those applying to the exemption from the hut tax—

The Kabaka will be granted exemption for 10 gun-bearers, and each of the recognised chiefs of an administrative sub-division shall be granted exemptions for five gun-bearers.

The above exemptions in relation to the gun-bearers, or the possession of guns, refer to guns which are used for private purposes. In addition to this, however, no gun licences will be levied on guns which are used by the Kabaka, or the other recognised chiefs of Ankole, for the purpose of arming a police force: provided that such native police force is instituted in accordance with the permission and under the control of the principal European officer administering the Ankole district for the British Government.

D. THE SUBSIDIARY AGREEMENT OF 1907

Kabula 22 August 1907.

We, the Kabaka and county chiefs of Ankole in baraza assembled resolve as follows:—

(*a*) We agree that a yearly payment of R2/- or one month's labour in lieu thereof shall in future take the place of all indefinite contributions and services hitherto due from the peasant to his Mutongole or chief;

(*b*) We agree that every Saza shall in future give one fifth of the 10 per cent rebate in hut tax he receives from Government to his Batongole:

the payments to the latter being made proportional to the sums they collect;

(c) We agree to set apart certain shambas for the purpose of food supply to chiefs and Batongole, the owners of such shambas being exempt from the payment of R 2/- or one month's labour described above.

KAHAYA. DUHARA.
BAGUTA. NYEMERA.
AZIZ. KAKULULU.
KABUTULU.
LIAMGWIZI.
A. EFFENDI.

Approved

GEORGE WILSON,
Acting Commissioner.

Signed in my presence

A. H. WATSON,
Acting Collector.

REFERENCES

Crazzolara, Father J. P. *The Lwoo, Part I,* Verona, 1950.

Fisher, Mrs. A. B. *Twilight Tales of the Black Baganda,* London, 1911.

Gorju, Rt. Rev. J. *Entre le Victoria, l'Albert et l'Edouard,* Rennes, 1920.

Gray, Sir J. M. "Early Treaties in Uganda, 1888-1891" *Uganda Journal,* Vol 12, pp. 25-42, 1948.

Kanyamunyu, P. K. "The Tradition of the Coming of the Abalisa Clan to Buhwezu, Ankole" *Uganda Journal,* Vol. 15, pp. 191-2, 1951.

Katate, A. G. and Kamugungunu, L. *Abagabe b'Ankole, Ekitabo I & II,* Eagle Press, Kampala, 1955.

Lukyn Williams, F. "Early Explorers in Ankole" *Uganda Journal,* Vol. 2, pp. 196-208, 1935.

Lukyn Williams, F. "Nuwa Mbaguta, Nganzi of Ankole" *Uganda Journal,* Vol. 10, pp. 124-35, 1946.

Morris, H. F. "The Kingdom of Mpororo" *Uganda Journal,* Vol. 19, pp. 204-7, 1955.

Morris, H. F. "The Making of Ankole" *Uganda Journal,* Vol. 21, pp. 1-15, 1957.

Morris, H. F. "The Murder of H. St. G. Galt" *Uganda Journal,* Vol. 24, pp. 1-15, 1960.

Nganwa, Kesi K. *Abakozire eby'Okutangaza Omuri Ankole,* Eagle Press, Nairobi, 1948.

Nicolet, Father J. *Mucondozi,* Mbarara, 1953.

Oliver, R. "Ancient Capital Sites of Ankole" *Uganda Journal,* Vol. 23, pp. 51-63, 1959.

Oliver, R. "The Baganda and the Bakonjo" *Uganda Journal,* Vol. 18, pp. 31-3, 1954.

INDEX